MW00559143

Kelley Wingate
Reading Comprehension and Skills

Sixth Grade

Credits
Content Editor: Christy M. Howard
Copy Editor: Beatrice Allen

Visit *carsondellosa.com* for correlations to Common Core, state, national, and Canadian provincial standards.

Carson-Dellosa Publishing, LLC
PO Box 35665
Greensboro, NC 27425 USA
carsondellosa.com

ISBN 978-1-4838-0497-2
02-249161151

Table of Contents

Introduction

Introduction

Reading proficiency is as much a result of regular practice as anything. This book was developed to help students practice and master the basic skills necessary to become competent readers.

The skills covered within the activity pages of this book are necessary for successful reading comprehension. Many of the activities will build and reinforce vocabulary, the foundation of reading comprehension. These activities lead to practice with more advanced comprehension skills. Then, students begin to answer comprehension questions based on specific reading passages.

The intent of this book is to strengthen students' foundation in reading basics so that they can advance to more challenging reading work.

Common Core State Standards (CCSS) Alignment

This book supports standards-based instruction and is aligned to the CCSS. The standards are listed at the top of each page for easy reference. To help you meet instructional, remediation, and individualization goals, consult the Common Core State Standards alignment chart on page 4.

Leveled Reading Activities

Instructional levels in this book vary. Each area of the book offers multilevel reading activities so that learning can progress naturally. There are three levels, signified by one, two, or three dots at the bottom of the page:

Level I: These activities will offer the most support.
Level II: Some supportive measures are built in.
Level III: Students will understand the concepts and be able to work independently.

All children learn at their own rate. Use your own judgment for introducing concepts to children when developmentally appropriate.

Hands-On Learning

Review is an important part of learning. It helps to ensure that skills are not only covered but internalized. The flash cards at the back of this book will offer endless opportunities for review. Use them for a basic vocabulary drill, or to play bingo or other fun games.

There is also a certificate template at the back of this book for use as students excel at daily assignments or when they finish a unit.

Common Core State Standards Alignment Chart

Common Core State Standards*		Practice Page(s)
Reading Standards for Literature		
Key Ideas and Details	6.RL.1–6.RL.3	5, 6, 8–11, 13, 15, 17–20
Craft and Structure	6.RL.4–6.RL.6	13, 15, 17–20, 101–103
Range of Reading and Level of Text Complexity	6.RL.10	5–7, 9–16, 18–20
Reading Standards for Informational Text		
Key Ideas and Details	6.RI.1–6.RI.3	21–33, 35–38, 40, 41, 43, 44, 46–48, 50–52, 54, 57, 58, 60, 62, 64, 66, 68, 70–74, 77–81, 83–85
Craft and Structure	6.RI.4–6.RI.6	21–33, 35, 41, 43, 54, 57, 58, 66, 68, 70–73, 84, 85
Integration of Knowledge and Ideas	6.RI.7–6.RI.9	58, 74, 77, 78, 80, 81, 83–85
Range of Reading and Level of Text Complexity	6.RI.10	34, 38, 39, 42, 44, 45, 49, 51–57, 59, 61, 63, 65, 67, 69, 75, 76, 79–83
Writing Standards		
Text Types and Purposes	6.W.1–6.W.3	8, 17
Production and Distribution of Writing	6.W.4–6.W.6	40, 46
Research to Build and Present Knowledge	6.W.7–6.W.9	8
Language Standards		
Conventions of Standard English	6.L.1–6.L.2	46
Vocabulary Acquisition and Use	6.L.4–6.L.6	86–103

Comprehension: Fiction

Read the passage. Then, answer the questions. Use information from the text to support your answers.

In the Dark

I need to get out! It's so dark in here. It's pitch-black—no light coming through any cracks. It's like a cave. I know I'm not alone here. Weight presses in on me from all directions. I may be thin, but this is ridiculous. It's been days since any light has entered. I have to get out. There's so much noise. Everyone wants out. That whiny Blue over there . . . complaining about being down here since August. What does he expect? No one wants a broken one. Crayons aren't any fun when they're in bits and pieces. That Number Two, she gets out every once in a while. I'm not sure she's gonna make it, though. Looks awfully rough when she gets back. I swear she's getting shorter, and look at those teeth marks! Everyone else, they think they're so important. I'm the important one, though. I'm worth credit. I was supposed to be handed in over eight days ago! I can count, you know. Numbers are my specialty. Oh, I see light! There's some rustling . . . there goes Number Two again, bypassed that pack of 16. Relief. I don't feel so squashed. A hand . . . It touched me! Ooooo, numbers, feels great to be doing what I was made to do. What? That's not the answer. Phone number!?!? OUCH! YEOW! What do you think you're doing? You can't have that. You get back here right now. Noooooooo! Darkness. I'll never get out of here.

Answer the questions and follow the directions. Highlight in the text where you found the information. Write the number of the question where you highlight.

1. Who is speaking in this piece? _____

2. What is the setting? _____
   Highlight the key words or phrases in the text with yellow.

3. Who or what is Blue? _____
   Highlight the key words or phrases in the text with blue.

4. Who is Number Two? _____

5. What is wrong with her? _____

6. What day of the week is it?   Monday   Wednesday   Friday   Saturday

7. What happens to the speaker at the end? _____

   _____

Comprehension: Fiction

Read the passage. Then, answer the questions. Use information from the text to support your answers.

An Ant's Life

Hal lugged the sandwich crumb through one tunnel after another. It was a relief to be out of the blazing sunlight. His downward journey was made in the company of thousands of his fellow six-footed colonists. He was tired—weary, but still going. He knew the need for food was all-important. Still, that story haunted him. The one about the grasshopper and the ant. Yes, they did have food to eat and a safe, warm home, but wasn't fun necessary, too? Hal had talked to Granny about it. "You can't fill your belly with fun or stay alive on daydreams," had been her reply. "Be happy with your existence." Hal walked slowly from the storage area, still depressed and thoughtful. A half hour wouldn't hurt, would it? He could grab extra crumbs during the rest of the day. He would still do his part. Besides, wouldn't he be more productive after having a little rest or a bit of fun? He looked towards the sunlit opening of the ant hill. A smile spread slowly across his face. There were plenty of detours available between the ant hill and that picnic.

1. What is the setting? _____

2. Who are the characters? _____

3. What does Hal call the other ants? _____

4. What is Hal's problem? _____

5. What is the cause of Hal's problem? _____

_____

6. Who did Hal talk to about his problem? How did that character respond? _____

_____

_____

7. Highlight with yellow the rationale for staying and working.

8. Highlight with green the rationale for having some fun.

9. What do you think Hal will do next? Why? _____

_____

Comprehension: Fiction

Read the letter. Then, answer the questions on page 8.

Dear Jeremy,

Remember last year when we learned how good ladybugs are for plants? We found out that they eat harmful insects like aphids and the cottony-cushion scale. Some gardeners and farmers even pay to have ladybugs shipped to them for plant protection. Just a few of these beetles can eat hundreds of harmful insects from one tree, reducing the need for pesticides.

Well, my mom (who usually loves having the oval, spotted insects around our garden) has a bit of a different opinion right now. You'll never believe what happened! Our house has become one huge ladybug mansion. Mom is going bonkers!

We learned in school that ladybugs love to crawl into leaves and cracks in trees. Well, I found out that cracks in houses will do, too! When I came home last Tuesday, the sides of our house and all the screens were covered with ladybugs. They even came inside the house through cracks and around the air conditioning unit upstairs. The upstairs ceiling was covered. I found about 70 of the bugs clustered behind a curtain on a window upstairs. My sister is having a ball trying to catch them in the bathroom. She has jars filled with the little crawlies.

Mom's been calling gardening stores and searching the Internet. She found out that the beetles are attracted to light-colored buildings, especially those warmed by the sun. Boy, is she rethinking that decision to paint the house white! Once they get inside, it's hard to get rid of ladybugs. If you disturb them, they secrete a nasty-smelling yellow liquid from their leg joints. Vacuuming them up is one solution. People should also check the siding and window openings and caulk any cracks around dryer vents, windows, etc. Mom has Dad recaulking any windows that look like they have openings big (or small) enough for those little buggers.

I managed to get extra credit in science and math from this! I did some research for my science report. I learned that the two-spotted ladybug is the most common. I decided to count the spots on some of our ladybugs. Of the 256 critters I looked at, fewer than 30 had one or two spots. In fact, 197 of them had more than six spots. I looked on the Internet and found out why. Here in the northern states, ladybugs have more spots because the darker spots help them retain more heat. Pretty interesting. Sure explained what was going on at my house.

Hope you have just dust bunnies, dirt, and some candy wrappers to vacuum up at your house. If you need an extra credit project, just stop over. See you soon.

Your friend,

Ian

Comprehension: Fiction

Use the letter on page 7 to help you answer the questions.

1. What other words does Ian use in place of the word "ladybugs" in his letter?
   List six of them here.

   _____   _____   _____

   _____   _____   _____

2. Why do you think the ladybugs chose Ian's house? Give two reasons. _____

   _____

   Highlight key words and phrases in the text with green.

3. What are two ways to get rid of unwanted ladybugs?

   _____   _____

4. How are ladybugs useful? _____

5. When do ladybugs become a nuisance? _____
   Highlight key words and phrases in the text with yellow.

6. How does Ian's mother feel about ladybugs? Explain your answer. _____

   _____

7. Why did the majority of Ian's ladybugs have more than six spots? _____

   _____

   _____

8. Where in the house did Ian and his family find ladybugs? Highlight four locations in the text with red.

9. In this passage, Ian has chosen to research ladybugs and write a letter to his friend Jeremy. Choose a topic to research and write a letter to your teacher about your findings.

Comprehension: Fiction

Read the interview. Then, answer the questions.

Each person in Yoriko's class was assigned to interview a professional and write a summary of the interview. Yoriko interviewed her optometrist, Dr. Iris.

Yoriko: I am interested in finding out how to care for your eyes if they have problems. What should you do if you get something in your eye? Rub it?

Dr. Iris: Never rub your eye if there is something in it. You could scratch your cornea. Pull your upper lashes gently out to lift your upper eyelid. Pull it very gently over your lower eyelashes. This can cause the object to fall out or your eyes to tear and wash out the object.

Yoriko: What if that doesn't work?

Dr. Iris: Then seek medical attention right away.

Yoriko: What if a chemical gets into your eye?

Dr. Iris: Immediately flush your eyes with warm water, preferably from a faucet, but you can also use a cup. Do this for at least 20 minutes. See a doctor or call the poison control center.

Yoriko: What should you do for a black eye?

Dr. Iris: Get a cool, wet washcloth. Press it gently on the eye for about 15 minutes every hour. It is a good idea to have a doctor check the eye for internal damage.

Yoriko: Okay, here's the gross one: what should you do if something cuts your eye or gets stuck in it?

Dr. Iris: The "getting stuck" is called penetration. If either of these things happen, DO NOT flush your eye, try to take out the object, or put any medicine on it. Gently cover the eye with gauze or a bandage and go straight to the nearest emergency room.

Yoriko: Thank you, Dr. Iris. I really learned a lot about caring for eyes.

Dr. Iris: You're welcome, Yoriko. It is important to take good care of your eyes. You only get one pair. Be sure to have your eyes checked once a year.

1. Help Yoriko with her summary. List four things Dr. Iris told her you could do when your eyes had a problem. Highlight words and phrases that support your answer.

_____

_____

_____

_____

2. Write a topic sentence for Yoriko's interview summary.

_____

Comprehension: Fiction

Have you ever heard of the "jar of life"? You only get to fill it once. Rocks are the most important things in life, like family and health. They are the things you cannot bear to live without. Pebbles are the next order of priorities: school, jobs, friends, and important items. Sand is the fun and the "stuff."

Read the poem. Then, answer the questions.

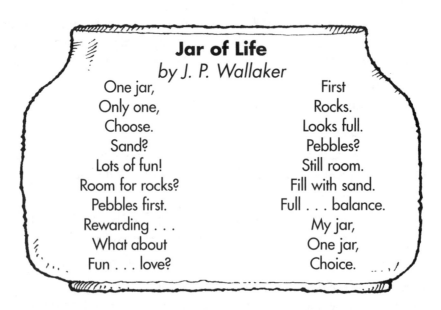

Jar of Life
by J. P. Wallaker

One jar,
Only one,
Choose.
Sand?
Lots of fun!
Room for rocks?
Pebbles first.
Rewarding . . .
What about
Fun . . . love?

First
Rocks.
Looks full.
Pebbles?
Still room.
Fill with sand.
Full . . . balance.
My jar,
One jar,
Choice.

1. What happens if you fill a jar with sand and then decide to drop in a rock? Use information from the text to support your answer.

_____

2. What is the main idea the author is trying to tell you about the little things in life?
   ○ They aren't important; you don't need them.
   ○ They are important but should not take the place of the important things in life.
   ○ They are the most important things of all.

3. In which order will you get the most of each in your jar?
   ○ rocks, then pebbles, then sand
   ○ pebbles, then rocks, then sand
   ○ sand, then rocks, then pebbles

4. Which statement best summarizes what the author is trying to say?
   ○ Going to the beach is fun. Sand is the thing!
   ○ Giving time to everything from those dear to you to fun is important, but it is essential to keep them in balance.
   ○ Only the "rocks" or things most important to you are essential.

Comprehension: Fiction

Read the passage. Then, answer the questions. Use information from the text to support your answers.

Milkweed

Maddie stood by the side of the road. She turned over yet another pale green leaf. No caterpillar. In her other hand, covered with sticky milky fluid, was a nearly empty ice cream bucket. One lone black, yellow, and white striped caterpillar was monotonously eating larger and larger swaths out of the leaf on the milkweed stem she had placed in there for its lunch. At this rate, she would need more leaves before leaving for school in the morning. Maddie looked up. She saw her friend Jade approaching. Jade parked her bike. "What'cha looking for?" she asked.

"I promised my teacher I would bring in five monarch caterpillars for our first science lesson this year. I've only found one so far." Jade put down her kickstand and began to help Maddie. She looked on several milkweed leaves, then moved over to look at the stem of a dandelion.

"Don't look there," said Maddie. "Monarch caterpillars only eat milkweed leaves. I've looked over this patch twice and can't find any more."

"No problem," Jade replied. "We have a huge patch of milkweed behind our house."

1. What is the setting? _____

_____

2. Who are the characters? Circle the name of each character once in the story.

3. What is the problem? _____

_____

4. What is your predicted solution? _____

   Highlight details in the story that helped you think of a solution.

5. Write two facts about monarch caterpillars.

_____

_____

Comprehension: Fiction

Read the journal entries. Then, complete the activities on page 13.

Kelli's Journal

Thursday—Shauna saw a scary movie about aliens last night. She said it was incredibly good. There were some kind of scary parts, she said, but they weren't too bad. Shauna didn't give me any details, because she didn't want to ruin the surprise for me. I just HAVE to see this movie! How can I convince my parents to let me see it? I've got to think of some good reasons for watching it.

Friday—I dropped some major hints today to my parents. I told them that there was this really great movie about aliens that we just had to see. I told them that it would be perfect for my brother Tony because he loves outer space. And after all, it's kind of educational too, right? We learn about the planets in science class. How could our parents not let us see it?? Mom said that if I cleaned my room and helped around the house, we could rent the movie tomorrow night. I can hardly wait! She said that when our rooms were done, Tony and I could each invite a friend over for the movie. I promised to do what she asked. I'm so excited!

Saturday morning—Kara's coming over tonight. Mom said she'd pick up the movie and some popcorn for us. Tony invited his friend Butch to come over. I hope they stay away from us. Can't wait to watch the movie, though!

Saturday night—Ugh! I will never sleep again! Kind of scary, but not too bad—who's Shauna kidding? The movie began with rows of aliens approaching the screen, ready to invade us. In the first five minutes, 17 different alien creatures popped out and I screamed at each one! I left and went to my room. Tony and his friend will spread it all over school. I'll never live it down. Even Kara called me a chicken afterwards. I can still hear the creepy theme music in my head....

Comprehension: Fiction

Use the journal entry on page 12 to complete the activities. Write the events in the correct sequence on the event chain.

a. Kelli and Tony invite Kara and Butch.

b. Kara calls Kelli a chicken.

c. Mom agrees to the movie.

d. Kelli cleans her room.

e. Kelli talks to her mom.

f. Shauna tells Kelli about the movie.

g. They begin watching the alien movie.

h. Shauna saw the *Alien Invasion* movie.

i. Kelli goes to her room.

j. Kelli watches five minutes of the movie.

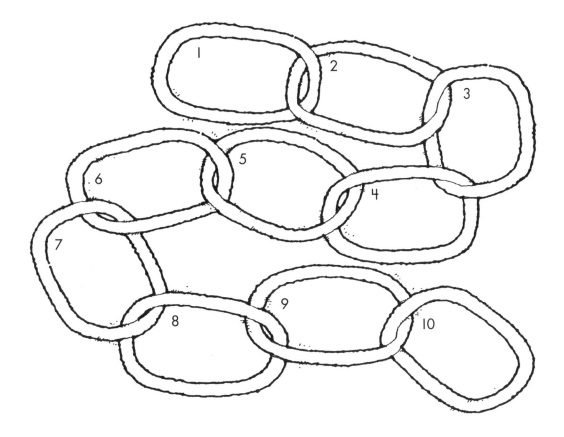

How would the final links change if an adjustment were made in link 7? Look at the change. Write three additional links to follow the new link.

Link 7: Kelli's parents decide that the kids need to choose a different movie.

Comprehension: Fiction

Read the text. Then, complete the activities on page 15.

Rolling Monsters

You are strapped in a seat. A padded bar comes down over your shoulders, allowing minimal movement. Your shoulder itches but you can't reach it. There is a sudden jerk, and you begin to move forward slowly. Your body tilts until you are looking straight up into a bank of clouds. Your body tenses. Anticipation causes your stomach to roil as you hear a steady "click, click, click" and slowly climb higher and higher. You reach the top, and the pause seems to last forever. You are catapulted forward, dropping down at a speed that forces the bile in your throat to return to your stomach. The passing wind slicks your hair back and brings tears to your eyes. The pressure stretches the skin on your face towards the back of your scalp. A lifetime of seconds and you are at the bottom, racing forward into a series of loops that won't allow your thinking brain to catch up to your emotional body. It's over. One hundred twenty seconds of adrenaline that lasted forever. You climb out of the seat on shaky legs. A relieved body and mind finally find each other. Go again? Of course. Back to the two-hour line.

Roller coasters are quick trips into total feeling and fear. Over 300 million people ride them each year to please peers or family members, to prove courage, or just for fun. Monster coasters tower over amusement parks worldwide.

Where did they come from? Russia. A country of many weather extremes found ice sledding a popular sport. In the 1400s, hills were built from wood frames and covered with hard-packed snow. Water was sprayed onto the snow to create a frozen downward pathway of increased speed. Some hills reached 70 feet high and were as steep as today's coasters. After a walk to the top, the customer rode down on a two-foot-long sled sitting on a guide's lap. Accidents did happen but the sport continued. In the 1700s, colorful lanterns allowed for night sledding in busy Saint Petersburg. People could not get enough of this sport, and wheels were added to the sleds to allow warm-weather riding.

In the 1800s, the ice slides moved to France. The warmer climate required some adjustments in thinking. Closely spaced rollers, like warehouse conveyors, were developed. The first wheeled coaster in Paris was opened in 1804. It was called the Russian Mountains. On this monster, small carriages whipped down a steep wooden hill. Many of the carriages jumped the track and caused injuries. As the years passed, more sophisticated and heart-stopping rides were developed.

Roller coasters today come in many shapes and sizes. They are found worldwide. Most people have ridden at least one and have certainly experienced the ride secondhand through television or video. Each rolling monster is out there just waiting for the chance to accelerate your heart rate.

Comprehension: Fiction

Use the passage on page 14 to complete the activities.

1. Write an alternative title for this article.

_____

2. What was the author's purpose in writing the first paragraph?

_____

3. Locate four descriptive verbs used in the story. Use each verb in a sentence of your own. Underline the verb in the sentence. Be sure to use proper capitalization, punctuation, and spelling.

_____

_____

_____

_____

4. Locate four descriptive adjectives used in the story. Use each adjective in a sentence of your own. Underline the adjective in the sentence. Be sure to use proper capitalization, punctuation, and spelling.

_____

_____

_____

Number the events below in the correct sequence from 1 to 6.

_____ Wheels were added to ice slide sleds.

_____ Russian Mountains was opened in Paris.

_____ Sophisticated rides were developed.

_____ In Russia, people made hills of wood frames covered with hard-packed snow.

_____ Ice slides moved to France.

_____ Colorful lanterns allowed night sledding in St. Petersburg.

Comprehension: Fiction

Read the passage. Then, answer the questions on page 17.

Find a Penny

Josh was walking to school with some of his friends. They saw a bright, shiny penny on the sidewalk. Josh stepped on it.

"Hey," said Anna. "Aren't you gonna pick it up?"

"Right," said Josh sarcastically. "'Find a penny pick it up, then all day you'll have good luck.' If it was a quarter, maybe . . ." He kicked it towards the sewer grate and they continued on their way.

They heard the first bell as they rounded the corner to the school. They started running. On the way up the steps, Josh wiped out and his backpack went flying. He limped down the hallway after Anna, Tio, and Zale. The last bell rang as Josh hit the door. "Tardy, Josh," said Ms. Clockswatch. "One more and you will have an extra assignment." The classroom phone rang. As Ms. Clockswatch turned her back to the doorway to answer it, Jade quietly slipped into the classroom and took her seat. She wiped her brow and gave a thumbs-up to Anna. She had narrowly escaped an extra assignment. "Let's begin by handing in our reading assignments," Ms. Clockswatch said as she turned back towards them. Josh pulled out his folder. His assignment was nowhere to be found! "But I spent three hours on it last night," he wailed.

The morning went from bad to worse. During a three-minute fact test, Josh's pencil lead fell out. Returning from the sharpener, he saw Jade put down her pencil and turn over her test. He wrote two answers and time was called. During science, his tray tipped over. Dirt, water, a plant, and science tools fell to the floor. An intercom announcement preceded the lunch bell. "The following students' artwork was selected for the City Art Fair: Haley Goodbrush, Gil Claymore, Jade Coinfinder . . ."

Jade requested a piece of pepperoni pizza. "Wow, huge slice!" she said. "Mmmm, looks good," thought Josh. He asked for one, too. "Sorry," said Mr. Vanfoods, "I just served the last one."

Josh flopped into a seat next to his friends. He eyed Jade's cheese-laden entrée. "You sure seem to be having a good day today," he muttered.

Jade laughed, "Yeah, you'll never guess what I picked up next to a sewer grate this morning . . ."

Name _____

Comprehension: Fiction

Use the passage on page 16 to answer the questions.

1. What kind of day is Josh having? _____
   Highlight specific details in the story that support your answer.

2. In what paragraph do you find the event that foreshadows Josh's day? _____

   _____

3. What kind of day is Jade having? _____
   Highlight three details in the story that support your answer.

4. What did Jade pick up? _____

5. What do you think Josh will do the next time he sees a penny? Explain your answer.

   _____

   _____

6. This passage tells us about Josh's bad day. Write a story about a bad day you have had. Be sure to use descriptive details to describe your event.

   _____

7. Number the events from 1 to 8 to put them in the correct sequence.

   _____ Josh misses out on pepperoni pizza.

   _____ Josh's science tray tips over.

   _____ Jade comes into class late.

   _____ Josh trips on the school steps.

   _____ An announcement is made that Jade's artwork will be in the City Art Show.

   _____ Josh kicks a penny.

   _____ Jade completes her math facts quiz.

   _____ Josh can't find his reading assignment.

Comprehension: Fiction

Read the passage. Then, answer the questions. Use information from the text to support your answers.

Theme Park

"Twenty-five, 50, 75, 80, 81, 82 . . . That's $47.82," counted Cal. He gathered the change and placed it next to the bills on the red comforter. Then he flopped back onto the bed, making the change bounce.

"Rats! We still need $13.28 to cover the admission cost," pouted Cleo. "Mom said we have to have the total cost of admission before we can go to the Greatest Theme Park Ever." The two lay on the twin beds in Cal's room, imagining the theme park: great junk food like chili dogs, cotton candy, frozen drinks, and elephant ears; grandstand games taking change and giving promises of brightly colored trinkets; and the rides, oh, the rides—wild roller coasters, water rides, and Ferris wheels.

"We won't have enough for two more weeks with our allowances," said Cal. "Besides, that doesn't leave anything for food or souvenirs."

"I know," Cleo whined, "and I've already checked between the couch cushions, under the car seats, and in all our jacket pockets." The two sat in mutual gloom. They watched the colorful leaves drop outside the window. Suddenly, an idea fell right into their greedy little heads.

1. What is the setting? _____

   _____

2. Who are the characters? Circle the name of each character once in the story.

3. What is the problem? _____

   _____

4. What is your predicted solution? _____

   _____

   Highlight details in the story that helped you think of a solution.

Comprehension: Fiction

Read the passage. Then, answer the questions. Use information from the text to support your answers.

Housefly

Swak! The flyswatter hit the table for yet another near miss. A fly buzzed tauntingly just above Jeffree's head. It relaxed and landed on the edge of the window. Smik! Julia tallied her tenth kill in a row. "Absolutely no way!" yelled Jeffree. "There is no way you can get those flies every time!"

"Good thing for you I can," said Julia. "You left the sliding door open and let all those flies come right into the house. You know Mom will have a fit if they're still in here at dinnertime." Smack! Julia landed another one as if to prove her point.

Swak! Swak! Swak! Jeffree missed three more, the sweat running down his face as much from effort as from the heat. "Okay, I give. How do you do it? Last week you couldn't hit a fly if it was the size of a bird. This week you can't miss."

"It's knowledge, you know," Julia said. "I checked out a book from the library and found out something interesting about these flies—they take off backwards."

"What!?"

"Backwards. When a fly takes off, it goes backwards, then shoots off forwards. If you aim right behind their little behinds, you get them every time."

Jeffree grinned as he eyed his latest prey.

1. What is the setting? _____

2. What is making the sounds "swak," "smik," and "smack"? _____

3. What event caused flies in the house? _____

4. Why is Julia able to hit the flies when Jeffree can't? _____

5. Who said, "What!?" How can you tell? _____

_____

6. What do you predict Jeffree will do next? Highlight the relevant details in the story. _____

_____

_____

Comprehension: Fiction

Read the passage. Then, answer the questions. Use information from the text to support your answers.

Waiting

Maddie stands alone outside by the side of the road, stamping her feet. The sky begins to turn a slate gray. There are no extra colors, not even a last minute spark of light. She looks longingly at her home. The lighted windows smile warmly out at her. Maddie rubs her hands together and blows on their bluing tips. "Should have grabbed my mittens," she thinks. A heavy weight rests in the middle of her back. Knowledge.

Shivering neighbors slide quietly into a circle of warmth. Too sleepy to talk, they share body warmth and protection from the wind. Barren trees stand guard as they wait. A pair of wide-spaced lights approaches. The circle stirs. It is a false alarm.

A few minutes later, another pair of lights shines like eyes in the dim light. A welcoming yellow haven stops and opens, admitting the chilly youngsters into humming warmth. It moves along its ebony ribbon, between the sentinel trees to other cold huddlers and a final destination that will open the mind.

1. What time of day is it? _____
   Highlight details that support your answer.

2. Why is Maddie standing by the road? _____
   Highlight details that support your answer.

3. Which two words best describe Maddie? Circle them.

   cold   wise   tired   fearful

4. Who are the shivering neighbors? _____

5. What actually made the circle stir the first time? _____

6. What things do the following phrases describe?

   "yellow haven" _____

   "destination that will open the mind" _____

   "ebony ribbon" _____

   "heavy weight . . . in the middle of her back" _____

Comprehension: Informational Text

Read the passage. Then, answer the questions. Use information from the text to support your answers.

Hammurabi's Code

One reason that modern countries run smoothly is that their laws are published. Because of this, all citizens know what laws they must follow. During ancient times, laws were not always recorded. A Babylonian king named Hammurabi created the first set of written laws for his people around 1760 BCE. He wanted to bring all of the people in his empire together under one set of laws. Because the laws were written down, everyone, whether rich or poor, was expected to obey them. Hammurabi's Code included 282 laws written in cuneiform, a type of writing in which symbols were carved into clay tablets. Each law included a penalty, or punishment, for disobeying it. The laws were written on a stela, which was a large slab of stone that was posted for all to see. Archaeologists working in the area now known as Iran discovered the stela in 1901. Spectators may view Hammurabi's Code in the Louvre Museum in Paris.

1. What is the main idea of this story?

    a. Modern countries publish their laws.

    b. Hammurabi's Code was an ancient set of laws.

    c. Archaeologists often find ancient materials.

2. Who was Hammurabi?

    _____

    _____

3. Why did Hammurabi write down his laws?

    _____

    _____

4. What is a *stela*?

    _____

5. Where did archaeologists find Hammurabi's Code?

    _____

Name _____

Comprehension: Informational Text

Read the passage. Then, answer the questions. Use information from the text to support your answers.

Athens and Sparta

Athens and Sparta were two important city-states in ancient Greece. A city-state is a region controlled by one city that is usually part of a larger cultural area. The citizens of both Athens and Sparta were ruled by elected assemblies. In addition, Athens had elected leaders called archons, while Sparta had kings who governed until they died or were overthrown. The people of Athens valued education and the arts and sciences. However, the people of Sparta focused on military life. Men in Sparta had to serve in the military from a young age, while men in Athens could choose whether to serve or not. The Greek city-states fought each other during the Peloponnesian War, from 431 to 404 BCE. Although Sparta defeated Athens, it was conquered later by the city of Thebes. Today, the city of Sparta is remembered for its military skill. In contrast, Athens is remembered for its philosophers and writers.

1. What is the main idea of this story?

    a. The city of Thebes was also located in Greece.

    b. Sparta's kings ruled until they died or were overthrown.

    c. Sparta and Athens were two very different city-states in ancient Greece.

2. What is a city-state?

    _____

    _____

3. How were the governments of ancient Athens and Sparta different?

    _____

4. How were the governments of ancient Athens and Sparta similar?

    _____

5. What is Athens remembered for today?

    _____

Comprehension: Informational Text

Read the passage. Then, answer the questions. Use information from the text to support your answers.

Alexander the Great

Alexander the Great was the son of a Macedonian king. He was born in 356 BCE. Alexander learned about Greek culture from his teachers, including the famous philosopher Aristotle. Alexander became king at age 20, when his father died. He spread the Greek culture to foreign areas covering over 22 million square miles (nearly 57 million square kilometers). Alexander was an unusual ruler because he allowed people in different areas to govern themselves as long as they followed Greek customs. Alexander's empire shared a common currency and language, and many cities were named Alexandria in his honor. People from different parts of the empire, such as the Middle East and India, began to share knowledge with each other. This led to great achievements in science and art. Alexander died at age 33, and his empire was split among three generals. Alexander's empire was later absorbed into the Roman Empire.

1. What is the main idea of this story?

    a. Alexander the Great was an important leader in ancient times.

    b. Alexander was the son of a Macedonian king.

    c. Aristotle was a great philosopher of ancient Greece.

2. How did Alexander learn about Greek culture?

    _____

3. What made Alexander an unusual leader?

    _____

4. What similarities did parts of Alexander's empire share?

    _____

    _____

5. What happened to Alexander's empire after his death?

    _____

6. What does *absorbed* mean?

    _____

Comprehension: Informational Text

Read the passage. Then, answer the questions. Use information from the text to support your answers.

The Silk Road

The Silk Road was not really a road, nor was it made out of silk. The Silk Road is the name used to refer to the route leading from Asia to the West. People traveled along this route to trade goods, including silk and spices from China and gold and silver from Rome, Italy. Few people traveled the entire distance of the Silk Road because it was several thousand miles long and very dangerous. The route included deserts and mountains, and there was always the danger of meeting bandits. People traded with each other along the way and took goods with them to others farther along. In addition to goods, ideas and inventions were also traded along the Silk Road. Some technological innovations that travelers brought from Asia to the West included the magnetic compass and the printing press. The Italian adventurer Marco Polo was one of many travelers along the Silk Road.

1. What is the main idea of this story?

    a. Many goods and ideas were traded along the Silk Road.

    b. The Silk Road was long and dangerous.

    c. Marco Polo traveled along the Silk Road.

2. What was the Silk Road?

    _____

    _____

3. What did people trade along the Silk Road?

    _____

    _____

4. Why did few people travel the entire distance of the Silk Road?

    _____

5. What were two technological innovations brought from Asia to the West?

    _____

Comprehension: Informational Text

Read the passage. Then, answer the questions. Use information from the text to support your answers.

The Tang Dynasty

For many years, China was governed by a series of dynasties, or rulers from the same family. The Tang Dynasty, which ruled from about AD 618 to 907, is considered China's Golden Age. Theater, dancing, sculpting, and painting were all very popular during this time. The capital city, Chang'an, had over one million people. Farmers were allowed to own land, although this later changed. People who wanted to work in the government had to pass a difficult exam. Only the smartest and most educated people could serve as government officials. The Tang government took a census to determine the empire's population, and households paid taxes on grain and cloth. Trade inside China and to other countries flourished because new roads and waterways made it easier to travel. Today, the Tang Dynasty is seen as a time of great cultural achievement.

1. What is the main idea of this story?

    a. The Tang government taxed grain and cloth.

    b. The Tang Dynasty lasted for nearly 300 years.

    c. The Tang Dynasty was a period of great cultural achievement.

2. What artistic activities were popular during the Tang Dynasty?

    _____

3. How did people become government officials?

    _____

4. Why did the government take a census?

    _____

5. What does it mean to *flourish*?

    _____

Comprehension: Informational Text

Read the passage. Then, answer the questions. Use information from the text to support your answers.

The Trail of Tears

    People of different cultures lived in North America before European explorers arrived. As Europeans began to settle the New World, they competed with Native Americans for land and other resources, such as gold. Over time, the New World was divided into states and a government was formed. The U.S. government passed laws in the 1830s making it legal to force Native Americans to relocate if settlers wanted their land. The Cherokee and other Native American groups had to move from the southeastern United States to lands farther west. Thousands of Native Americans traveled over 1,000 miles (1,600 kilometers) on foot from their homelands to the land that later became the U.S. state of Oklahoma. Many people died from disease or hunger along the route. The name "Trail of Tears" was given to this event in U.S. history because of the struggles people faced on their journeys. Today, the descendants of the survivors of the Trail of Tears make up the Cherokee Nation.

1. What is the main idea of this story?

    a. Many people from Europe settled in the New World.

    b. Some Native Americans still live in Oklahoma today.

    c. The Trail of Tears was a forced relocation of Native Americans in the United States.

2. What did European settlers compete with Native Americans for?

    _____

3. How did the U.S. laws that were passed in the 1830s affect Native Americans?

    _____

4. Where were Native Americans forced to move?

    _____

5. What is the Trail of Tears?

    _____

    _____

    _____

Comprehension: Informational Text

Read the passage. Then, answer the questions. Use information from the text to support your answers.

Photosynthesis

Photosynthesis is the process in which plants use sunlight to produce food and oxygen. In addition to light, plants need water and carbohydrates to grow. A plant gathers water through its roots. It also takes in carbon dioxide from the air. A compound called chlorophyll helps plants use sunlight. Chlorophyll is what makes plants green. Plants use energy from the sun to break down the water and carbon dioxide. Through photosynthesis, plants produce oxygen and glucose. Glucose is a type of sugar that plants use for energy. Some people refer to trees as the "lungs of the planet." This is because trees help keep a balance between oxygen and carbon dioxide in the air. When people or animals breathe in oxygen, they exhale carbon dioxide. Plants convert carbon dioxide into oxygen that people and animals can breathe.

1. What is the main idea of this story?

    a. People and animals breathe in oxygen.

    b. Plants use energy from the sun.

    c. Photosynthesis is a process that helps plants produce food and oxygen.

2. What do plants need to grow?

    _____

3. What makes plants green?

    _____

4. What is glucose?

    _____

    _____

5. Why are trees sometimes called the "lungs of the planet"?

    _____

    _____

Name _____

Comprehension: Informational Text

Read the passage. Then, answer the questions. Use information from the text to support your answers.

Chambered Nautilus

The chambered nautilus is a modern living fossil. It is related to the cephalopods: octopuses, squids, and cuttlefish. Unlike its cousins, the nautilus has an external shell. The shell is made up of many chambers. The animal lives in the outermost chamber and uses the rest to regulate its buoyancy, or ability to sink and float. The chambered nautilus lives in the Indian and South Pacific Oceans. It finds its home at depths from 60 to 1,500 feet along reef walls. On dark, moonless nights, it travels closer to the surface to eat tiny fishes, shrimp, and the molted shells of spiny lobsters. The chambered nautilus cannot change color or squirt ink like its relatives, but it does have arms. Two rows of 80 to 100 small tentacles surround its head. None have suckers to hold prey, but each can touch and taste. The nautilus lives longer than other cephalopods, sometimes up to 20 years. Unlike the octopus, it mates many times during its lifetime, each time attaching eggs to rocks, coral, or the seafloor. Each egg takes a year to hatch. Humans are the main threat to this ancient creature's continued survival. Well over 5,000 living nautiluses are harvested each year to supply shell dealers.

1. Where do chambered nautiluses live? _____

_____

2. Define a *chambered nautilus*. _____

_____

3. What do nautiluses eat? _____

_____

4. What happens to nautilus eggs? _____

_____

5. Highlight how nautiluses are the same as other cephalopods with yellow.
   Write one similarity here. _____

6. Highlight how nautiluses are different from other cephalopods with green.
   Write one difference here. _____

_____

Comprehension: Informational Text

Read the passage. Then, complete the activities on pages 30 and 31.

Touchpoints

Your brain is constantly making pathways and interconnecting experiences. This allows you to access vivid mental images, emotions, or even smells when you hear about, think about, or read about certain events. When you think of the word "sister" or "brother," a mental image immediately comes to mind. An emotion may also register, especially if your sister just did something nasty. Think about the word "pond." Each person gets a mental picture based on her own experience. Does yours have a white sandy beach or is grass growing down to the water's edge? Is the water clear and blue, or is the surface covered with lily pads and duckweed?

Your understanding is influenced by the previous knowledge you have tucked away into mental file cabinets. Being aware of these connecting experiences increases our understanding of new experiences. This is especially true when it comes to understanding what we read; all of our past knowledge impacts what we comprehend.

This knowledge can come from personal experience, things we have seen in electronic format, other books, or information someone else has shared with us. Each time a tie, or reference, is made between bits of mental information, it provides additional routes for retrieving it again from the billions of thoughts that have passed into our mental haystacks. Look at the example of Meg, who read two different books about boys living in the wilderness. As she was reading, Meg thought about times she had spent in woodland environments hunting with her dad, hiking with friends, or canoeing. She also thought about all of the movies, both fact and fiction, that she had seen in the past. A newscast about a missing teen also came into play, as well as numerous books Meg had read over the years. Each connection helped Meg become more involved in each book and increased her understanding and enjoyment of the two books.

1. Highlight with red four specific details about mental connections or touchpoints in the article.

2. Highlight with yellow the four places from which the past knowledge for mental connections can come.

Comprehension: Informational Text

Look at the entries Meg made in her Mental Connections chart. Use the information from her chart to complete the activity below.

Event in Text	Mental Connection
Pete, the boy in the story, talks about being hungry. He finds a berry patch and picks some berries to eat. Pete talks about how tasty they are. Later, however, he gets a stomachache from eating only berries.	This reminds me of my family. Every summer we pick strawberries, raspberries, and blueberries. I know how long it can take to pick them and how delicious they are when you are hungry. Getting a stomachache is also a familiar feeling. Too many berries on an empty stomach—ouch!
Pete needs to find shelter. He looks around, but there isn't much to be found in the wilderness. He becomes panicky; he wasn't prepared to live in the wild. He finally finds a cave-like opening he can make into a place to sleep.	This reminds me of the last book I read. In that book, Neil also needs to find shelter. The difference is, he had done some research on living in the wild. I'll bet that Pete would appreciate some of Neil's books.
Pete is found. He is glad to be going home. He is also very proud that he was able to survive on his own for three months.	Learning from a difficult situation . . .

1. Look at the first entry. List two specific parallel connections.

   text: _____

   Meg: _____

   text: _____

   Meg: _____

2. To what did Meg connect the first event? Circle your answer.

   another text   a personal experience

   a news incident   a TV program

3. What did Neil have that Meg believes Pete would like? _____

4. Why does she think this? Use information from the text to support your answer. _____

5. Complete the last entry in the chart under "Mental Connection." _____

6. Based on how it is used in the last paragraph of the passage, define *retrieving*. _____

Comprehension: Informational Text

Use this chart with the next text you read. List specific events from the text that trigger connecting memories or touchpoints. Write each event in detail in a separate box in the first column. Write the connecting memory in the second column. Be specific. Where did the memory come from?

Touchpoints

Title: _____

Author: _____

Event in Text	Mental Connection

Attribute Checklist

_____ evidence of reading book

_____ one event per box

_____ detailed events

_____ specific mental connections

Comprehension: Informational Text

Read the passage. Then, answer the questions. Use information from the text to support your answers.

Migration

Some animals migrate, or move, to different areas during different seasons. They may go to warmer climates during the winter and cooler climates during the summer. Some whales swim to Hawaii in the autumn to give birth to their young in warm waters. Then, they travel to Alaska in the summer. Salmon begin their lives in freshwater streams and travel to the ocean as adults. Their bodies change so that they can survive in saltwater. When it is time to lay eggs, salmon swim back to the freshwater streams where they were born. Monarch butterflies fly thousands of miles every autumn, from the northern United States to Mexico. In the spring, they fly north again. Many birds also migrate every year. The arctic tern has the farthest journey, traveling over 22,000 miles (32,000 km) from the Arctic Circle at the North Pole to Antarctica at the South Pole.

1. What is the main idea of this story?

   a. Some animals migrate at different seasons of the year.

   b. The arctic tern migrates over 22,000 miles a year.

   c. Hawaii has warmer waters than Alaska.

2. List one reason why animals might migrate.

   _____

   _____

3. Define *migrate*.

   _____

   _____

4. Where do monarch butterflies migrate every autumn?

   _____

5. Which animal has the farthest migration each year?

   _____

Comprehension: Informational Text

Read the passage. Then, answer the questions. Use information from the text to support your answers.

Fireflies

Fireflies are bioluminescent insects. This means they can produce their own light. They do this by mixing chemicals in their bodies. One chemical is common to all living things; it is called ATP. The other two chemicals are luciferin and luciferase. When all three are mixed with oxygen, the firefly is able to light its lantern, or the rear part of its body. The purpose of this light is to help find a mate. Each species of firefly has a specialized code. The code is made up of the number and length of flashes, the time between flashes, and the flight pattern while flashing. After mating, the female firefly lays about 100 eggs. Several days later, the female dies. When the eggs hatch, larvae emerge. The larvae are bioluminescent and sometimes called glowworms. The larvae eat during the spring, summer, and autumn months, sleep through two winters, and then progress into the next stage of their lives. They crawl into the soil, where they metamorphose, or change, into pupas. After about two months, they emerge as adult fireflies.

Firefly light is not hot. It is, however, very bright. Catching a few fireflies and putting them in a jar (with air holes) produces enough light to read in the dark. In some countries, fireflies are caught in nets and used as lanterns. People also use fireflies in festivals and wear them in small containers as jewelry.

1. What is the topic of this article? _____

2. Define bioluminescent. _____

   How does this relate to fireflies? _____

3. How do fireflies produce light? _____

4. What is the purpose of this light? _____

5. The firefly life cycle has four stages. Name them. Give one detail for each stage.

   _____

   _____

   _____

   _____

6. What uses have people had for fireflies? _____

   _____

Comprehension: Informational Text

Read the passage. Then, answer the questions on page 35.

Matter Study Sheet

Matter takes up space and has mass.

Two objects cannot occupy the same space at the same time.

There are three states of matter: solid, liquid, and gas.

> solid: certain size, shape, takes up space, has mass
> liquid: certain size, shape of container, takes up space, has mass
> gas: size and shape of container, takes up space, has mass

Matter has physical properties such as flexibility, color, texture, buoyancy, smell, mass, weight, shape, and size.

Liquid + liquid: mix together, solution, or separate into levels (remember food coloring in water and column of liquids)

Solid + liquid: sink, melt, dissolve, float, or become soggy

A physical change is a change in shape, size, or state but NOT in type of matter.

> Examples of physical changes to water:

> > divide water into 2 or more containers
> > freeze the water (change from liquid to solid)
> > melt ice (change from solid to liquid)
> > boil water (change from liquid to gas)
> > condensation (change from gas to liquid)
> > add a substance to it, forming a mixture (remember adding pepper, rice, etc.)
> > crush ice

A chemical change is a change in type of matter.

> Example: baking

Determine mass based on position of pan on a pan balance or ruler on ruler balance.

> Example: The apple has more mass because the pan is lower.

Give evidence that an item has volume. When placing an item in water, the water will rise. The difference can be measured to determine the volume.

A mixture is a combination of various types of matter in which each maintains its own properties and can be separated out (with tweezers, filter paper, sieve, etc.).

A solution is a mixture of two or more substances that cannot be separated by mechanical means (with tweezers, filter paper, sieve, etc.).

Comprehension: Informational Text

Use the information from the study sheet on page 34 to help you answer the questions.

1. What two characteristics do all states of matter share?

   _____   _____

2. Based on the information given, which state of matter are the following materials?

   pepper _____   air _____

   apple cider _____   chocolate chip _____

   water vapor _____   milk _____

3. Give one more example of each state of matter.

   solid: _____

   liquid: _____

   gas: _____

4. What principle of matter does this passage demonstrate? Two students, coming from opposite directions, run around a corner and crash into each other. Both end up staggering backwards.

   _____

   Write another example of this principle.

   _____

5. List two ways you could cause a physical change to occur to this paper.

   _____   _____

6. Are you made of matter? Give evidence to support your answer.

   _____

7. You have a bowl of trail mix. It contains pretzels, raisins, peanuts, oat cereal, and chocolate chips. Is it a mixture or a solution? _____

8. Define *physical* change.

   _____

Comprehension: Informational Text

Read the passage. Then, answer the questions. Use information from the text to support your answers.

Turn Up the Power

The ability to do work is called energy. Machines need energy or fuel to work. This energy can come from many sources. Fossil fuels like coal, gas, and oil are one important source of energy. They come from the earth and are used to fuel power plants, automobiles, and other machines. Another source of energy is wind. Wind can power windmills. It can also be converted into electricity, push gears to grind grains, or be used to pump water. Water is another key source of energy. Dams are used to harness energy from rivers and convert it into electricity. Scientists are also researching the possibility of using ocean waves and tides for energy. Finally, there is the sun, or solar energy. Solar cells can change sunlight into electricity, which can then be used to power cars, heat homes, and power electrical devices. Although fossil fuels are currently used the most, other energy sources are being used and research is being done to make them more effective and economical.

Write the topic and the main idea on the lines. Then list four major supporting details. Choose two minor supporting details for each and list them.

Topic: _____

Main idea: _____

1. Major supporting detail: _____

    A. Minor supporting detail: _____

    B. Minor supporting detail: _____

2. Major supporting detail: _____

    A. Minor supporting detail: _____

    B. Minor supporting detail: _____

3. Major supporting detail: _____

    A. Minor supporting detail: _____

    B. Minor supporting detail: _____

4. Major supporting detail: _____

    A. Minor supporting detail: _____

    B. Minor supporting detail: _____

Name _____

Comprehension: Informational Text

Read the passage. Then, answer the questions. Use information from the text to support your answers.

Fossils

   Fossils are the remains of plants or animals from thousands of years ago that have turned to stone. After these organisms died, their bodies were buried in sediment and gradually replaced by minerals. Sometimes an animal's bones, teeth, or shell are preserved. Other times only an impression of its body is made. Footprints, eggs, and nests can also be fossilized. Fossils can be found in many places. They are often uncovered when people dig up the earth as they build roads. Many fossils are buried in layers of rock. Sometimes, fossils are exposed through erosion of a mountainside. Others are found through undersea excavation. Scientists study fossils to learn what the living animals or plants looked like. They can use radiocarbon dating to find out how old a fossil is. All living things contain carbon, so scientists measure how much carbon is left in a fossil to determine its age.

1. What is the main idea of this story?

   a. Fossils can be found in many places.

   b. Sometimes only an impression of a plant is left.

   c. Fossils are plant or animal remains from long ago.

2. What happens when something is fossilized?

   _____

3. What parts of an animal's body might be preserved?

   _____

4. Why do scientists study fossils?

   _____

5. How does radiocarbon dating help scientists determine a fossil's age?

   _____

   _____

© Carson-Dellosa • CD-104624

37

Comprehension: Informational Text

Bamboo

What do you know about bamboo? Before you read the article on pages 39 and 40, read each pair of statements. Write a **P** before the statement you predict is true based on your prior knowledge. Then read the article on the next two pages. Review your choices. Write a **V** in front of each verified answer. Write the number of the paragraph that contains the answer.

1. _____ a. There are about 100 species of bamboo.

   _____ b. There are over 1,000 species of bamboo.

   Answer found in paragraph _____

2. _____ a. Bamboo is a grass.

   _____ b. Bamboo is a tree.

   Answer found in paragraph _____

3. _____ a. Bamboo flowers once a year.

   _____ b. Bamboo may take 80 years to flower.

   Answer found in paragraph _____

4. _____ a. Bamboo is grown only in China.

   _____ b. Bamboo is grown in both tropical and temperate climates.

   Answer found in paragraph _____

5. _____ a. Steel has a greater tensile strength than bamboo.

   _____ b. Bamboo has a greater tensile strength than steel.

   Answer found in paragraph _____

6. _____ a. One species of bamboo can grow up to 10 feet a day.

   _____ b. One species of bamboo can grow up to 4 feet a day.

   Answer found in paragraph _____

7. _____ a. Bamboo can be harvested faster than rattan or softwoods.

   _____ b. Rattan can be harvested faster, but bamboo grows larger.

   Answer found in paragraph _____

8. _____ a. Bamboo can be used to make paper, rebar, and food preservatives.

   _____ b. Bamboo can be used to make paper but not rebar or preservatives.

   Answer found in paragraph _____

9. _____ a. Thomas Edison used bamboo in his lightbulb experiment.

   _____ b. Thomas Edison used bamboo in his telephone experiment.

   Answer found in paragraph _____

Comprehension: Informational Text

Bamboo

When bamboo comes to mind, so, too, do images of pandas and China. While this plant is well known for its role in the life cycle of China's endangered pandas, it is now becoming known for its own deterioration.

Bamboo is a woody plant, but it is not a tree. It belongs to the grass family. It is the fastest growing plant on this planet. One species can grow up to four feet in 24 hours. It grows more than 30% faster than the fastest growing tree. There are over 1,000 species of bamboo. They are divided into two main types determined by their rhizome, or root, structures. Sympodial bamboos have clumps of roots and are commonly called "clumpers"; monopodial bamboos have roots that are runners and are commonly called "runners." Clumpers tend to grow in tropical climates while runners grow in temperate climates.

These fast growing plants share a unique characteristic: they rarely bloom. Each species blooms only once every 7 to 120 years, not every year like most plants. Most bamboo of the same species blooms at approximately the same time. Usually the parent plant dies soon after flowering.

Bamboo is delicate when it first emerges from the ground but soon becomes one of the most hardy plants around. The plant craves water when first planted, but within a year it can be somewhat drought tolerant. It also tolerates precipitation extremes from 30 to 250 inches of rainfall a year. One grove of bamboo even withstood the atomic blast at Hiroshima and within days sent up new shoots. It was the first regreening in that devastated area.

Bamboo has many uses. It grows fast, with some types reaching a mature height in just two months. India, China, and Burma have found that a grove of bamboo can be harvested and make a profit in as little as 3 to 5 years. This is much better than rattan, which takes 8 to 10 years to make a profit, and most softwoods, generally grown in the U.S. and Canada, which cannot be harvested for 10 to 20 years.

Bamboo is an excellent building material. It is pliable and one of the strongest building materials there is. In fact, its tensile strength is greater than steel's. Steel has a tensile strength of 23,000 psi, while bamboo's tensile strength is a superior 28,000 psi. Bamboo is also an excellent structural material for buildings in earthquake areas. In fact, after the violent 1992 earthquake in Limón, Costa Rica, only the National Bamboo Project's bamboo houses were left standing.

The history of electric lights owes much to bamboo. Thomas Edison used bamboo during his first experiment with the lightbulb. He used a piece of carbonized bamboo for the filament, or the part that glows to make light. It worked. Light was produced.

Comprehension: Informational Text

Soil conservation is another use of bamboo. Because it becomes established quickly, it can be planted in deforested areas that have trouble with erosion. Its dense root systems hold soil in place. It can also be used to strengthen areas of land that are prone to mudslides and earthquakes.

Bamboo is used to make many items we use daily. Bamboo pulp is used to make paper. Makes you wonder if this paper originated from a tree or a grass, doesn't it? It is also used to make paneling, floor tiles, briquettes for fuel, and rebar to reinforce concrete beams. An antioxidant in pulverized bamboo bark helps prevent the growth of bacteria. This is commonly used as a natural food preservative, especially in the country of Japan.

Pandas need bamboo; it may be essential to their survival. Bamboo needs each and every one of us. When we learn to use it to its full potential, we will no longer have to watch it deteriorate or fear that it will become as endangered as the panda.

Write a summary of this article. Craft your summary statement so that each detail sentence fits the focus.

_____

_____

_____

_____

_____

_____

_____

_____

_____

_____

Comprehension: Informational Text

Read the passage. Then, answer the questions. Use information from the text to support your answers.

Biomes of the World

Biomes are areas of land or water that share the same climate. Earth has several major biomes. Deserts receive little rain and have extreme temperatures. Forests receive more rain and have moderate temperatures. The trees in a deciduous forest lose their leaves every autumn. The trees in the taiga are mostly evergreens, many of which have needle-like leaves. Grasslands cover the most area of land on Earth. Rain is usually seasonal, so there is a dry season during which dust storms may be created. The tundra is located at very high elevations and near the North and South Poles. Few plants grow in the tundra, and the ground is permanently frozen. There are two types of aquatic biomes: marine and freshwater. Marine biomes cover about three-fourths of Earth's surface and include all of the world's oceans. Freshwater biomes are bodies of water such as lakes, rivers, and ponds.

1. What is the main idea of this story?

   a. Some biomes receive little rain.

   b. Deserts can be very hot or very cold.

   c. Earth has many different biomes.

2. What are biomes?

   _____

3. How are deserts and forests different?

   _____

   _____

4. What do many evergreens look like?

   _____

5. What happens during the dry season in the grasslands?

   _____

Comprehension: Informational Text

Read the passage. Then, answer the questions on page 43. Use information from the text to support your answers.

Go, Bones!

Most preteens do not worry about what their bodies will be like after they turn 40 or 50. After all, that's OLD!! Yet there are some very simple things that can be done before age 18 that will have a huge impact on life after 50. It is as simple as exercising, eating right, and getting plenty of calcium and vitamin D, which is needed for calcium absorption.

So what's the big deal? Osteoporosis—a big word that means bones are losing mass and are more apt to break or fracture. Osteoporosis can even cause collapsed vertebrae, resulting in incredible back pain and spinal deformities like a rounded back. About half of the women and one third of the men over 50 have osteoporosis. Over 20 million Americans and over 1.4 million Canadians suffer from this condition.

Osteoporosis cannot be cured. It can be treated, but not always successfully. The best way to take care of it is to prevent it. The best time to prevent it is before the age of 18. From birth to the late teens, people build their greatest amount of bone mass. This is the time when dietary calcium—from food instead of pills—directly results in bones growing to their maximum density. If bone mass is not built during this time, it cannot be "caught up" later.

The problem is that many children are not getting enough calcium in their diets. Milk and other dairy products are rich in calcium. Several studies have shown that girls and boys who drink lots of soft drinks and fruit beverages tend to drink less milk. Other studies have shown that drinking cola and caffeinated beverages leaches calcium out of the bones, meaning that more calcium is needed to compensate. Depending on the amount of caffeine, that can mean anywhere from one to five servings of calcium being leached from the bones.

Most adults need about 1000 mg of dietary calcium per day, without drinking cola; children need slightly more. People under 18 need the equivalent of four to five glasses of milk each day. For those who don't like milk, the good news is calcium can also be found in other foods like yogurt, cheese, and some green vegetables. In fact, if you start checking labels, you will be surprised where calcium shows up.

Other preventative measures include regular exercise, a balanced diet, and no smoking. The good news is you have the power to take preventative measures now. Armed with knowledge, you can have a direct impact on what your own life will be like when you become "old."

Comprehension: Informational Text

Use the article on page 42 to answer each question. Verify your answers in the text.

1. What is osteoporosis? _____

_____

2. List two possible consequences of a person over 50 getting osteoporosis. _____

_____

3. Why should kids be concerned about osteoporosis? _____

4. When is the most bone mass grown? _____

5. Why is milk important to this issue? _____

_____

6. What if you do not like to drink milk? _____

_____

7. What effect do caffeinated beverages have on the bones? _____

_____

8. What, besides calcium, will strengthen your bones and help prevent osteoporosis?

_____

9. Evaluate your own lifestyle. What could you do to help your bones? _____

_____

10. What is the main idea of the passage? _____

_____

_____

Comprehension: Informational Text

Penguins

What do you know about penguins? Before you read the article, read each pair of statements. Write a **P** before the statement you predict is true based on your prior knowledge. Then read the article on the next two pages. Review your choices. Write a **V** in front of each verified answer. Write the number of the paragraph(s) that contains the answer.

1. _____ a. All penguins live in Antarctica.

 _____ b. All penguins live south of the equator.

 Answer found in paragraph _____

2. _____ a. Not all penguins are endangered.

 _____ b. All penguins are endangered.

 Answer found in paragraph _____

3. _____ a. Penguins have hollow bones.

 _____ b. Penguins have dense bones.

 Answer found in paragraph _____

4. _____ a. The king penguin is the largest species of penguins.

 _____ b. The emperor penguin is the largest species of penguins.

 Answer found in paragraph _____

5. _____ a. Penguin ancestors were some of the best fliers in the world.

 _____ b. Penguin ancestors were some of the best walkers in the world.

 Answer found in paragraph _____

6. _____ a. Penguins can hold their breath underwater for over 15 minutes.

 _____ b. Penguins can hold their breath underwater for about 10 minutes.

 Answer found in paragraph _____

7. _____ a. Penguins have thick, coarse, waterproof hair instead of feathers.

 _____ b. Penguin feathers are covered with waterproofing body oil.

 Answer found in paragraph _____

8. _____ a. A penguin's camouflage helps it stay hidden in the ocean.

 _____ b. A penguin's camouflage helps it stay hidden in the snow.

 Answer found in paragraph _____

9. _____ a. Male penguins are the only ones that care for the chicks.

 _____ b. Both parents share the responsibilities of raising the chicks.

 Answer found in paragraph _____

10. _____ a. Penguins can be found in the wild in Canada and Japan.

 _____ b. Penguins can be found in the wild in New Zealand and South America.

 Answer found in paragraph _____

Comprehension: Informational Text

Penguins

Penguins are interesting creatures. There are over 16 different kinds of penguins, each with its own special characteristics. However, all penguins have certain things in common. Did you know that all of these birds are located in the Southern Hemisphere? Although some live in Antarctica, not all do. Each of these birds is located in coastal areas south of the equator.

Penguins possess unique adaptations. For instance, all penguins have dense bones. Hollow bones enable most birds to fly; dense bones help penguins travel through water. Penguins also have small, tightly packed outer feathers that are covered with a special body oil to make them waterproof. Beneath the outer feathers is the down, or fluffy feathers. Under the skin is a thick layer of fat. If a penguin gets too hot, it will fluff its feathers, allowing body heat to escape. Some penguin varieties can hold their breath for nearly 20 minutes while searching for food in the southern oceans. Their mouths are filled with rough spines which help hold their diet of slippery fish, squid, and crustaceans. Their webbed feet act like small wings to assist propulsion on these excursions.

Penguins have predators which are uncommon for most birds. They include sharks, killer whales, and leopard seals. Therefore, penguins have developed a unique form of camouflage. When seen from below, their white bellies help them blend in with the sun shining on the water; when seen from above, their dark backs help them fade into the dark ocean depths.

Many penguins lay and hatch eggs in large groups called rookeries or colonies. The hen (female) lays one to two eggs, and both the hen and the cock (male) share chick-raising duties. Adult penguins have a brood patch, a featherless spot on the underside, which allows their bodies to heat the incubating eggs or newly hatched chicks. When both parent penguins are at sea catching dinner for the little ones, the chicks may stay in a crèche, or nursery, where chicks gather for warmth and safety.

Researchers believe penguins may have been birds of flight at some time in the past. Today's penguins have evolved from seabirds called tubenoses who have nostrils located at the end of a tube on top of their beaks. Tubenoses include some of the greatest fliers in the world: albatrosses and petrels. It is believed that the earliest penguins branched from tubenoses about the time dinosaurs disappeared. The largest penguin fossil ever discovered was 5'7" tall. The *Anthropornis nordenskjoeldi* weighed nearly 300 pounds. Today's penguins are not nearly so large. The largest is the emperor penguin which stands over 3 feet tall and weighs up to 88 pounds. The second largest is the king penguin, standing about as tall as the emperor penguin but weighing only half as much.

Comprehension: Informational Text

All penguins in the wild today live between the equator and the South Pole. Their populations are counted in breeding pairs. Macaroni penguins account for nearly half of all penguins. They have about 11.8 million breeding pairs. Two species of Pacific Ocean penguins, the Galapagos and Humboldt penguins, are considered threatened with between 5,000 and 8,500 breeding pairs. The yellow-eyed penguin in New Zealand is an endangered species with as few as 1,600 breeding pairs.

Penguins are unusual birds. Adapted to aquatic life, their body composition and camouflage set them apart from their feathered, air-traveling cousins. Each penguin is unique, and people who cannot enjoy them in their Southern Hemispheric habitats can enjoy them in zoos or through electronic media.

Write a summary of this article. Craft your summary statement so that each detail sentence fits the focus. Be sure to use proper capitalization, punctuation, and spelling.

_____

_____

_____

_____

_____

_____

_____

_____

_____

_____

Comprehension: Informational Text

Read the passage. Then, answer the questions. Use information from the text to support your answers.

Eclipses

An eclipse happens when Earth and the moon line up with the sun. A lunar eclipse occurs when Earth moves between the sun and the moon. Earth blocks some sunlight from reaching the moon, so the moon appears dark from Earth's shadow. A solar eclipse occurs when the moon moves between Earth and the sun. The moon blocks some sunlight from reaching Earth, so the sky grows dark. It is safe to view a lunar eclipse, but you should never look directly at a solar eclipse, even through sunglasses. Instead, make a pinhole projector. Cut a small square in the middle of a piece of cardboard. Place a piece of aluminum foil across it, and then poke a small hole in it so that the sun's light will shine onto another piece of cardboard. You can safely look at the sun's image on the second piece of cardboard.

1. What is the main idea of this story?

   a. You should never look directly at the sun.

   b. An eclipse happens when sunlight is blocked by Earth or the moon.

   c. The sky grows dark during a solar eclipse.

2. When does a lunar eclipse occur?

   _____

   _____

3. What does the moon look like during a lunar eclipse?

   _____

4. When does a solar eclipse occur?

   _____

   _____

5. How can you safely look at a solar eclipse?

   _____

Comprehension: Informational Text

Read the passage. Use information from the text to complete the graphic organizer.

Infectious Disease

Viral infectious disease can be as frightening today as it was in the past when it meant probable death. Viral diseases are contagious. When they are not contained, they can become a health hazard. An epidemic is an infectious disease that affects a large number of people. The infection spreads outside of a limited group and lasts for a long time. The plague or "Black Death," spread through fleas infected by black rats, is one example of an epidemic. A pandemic is even more widespread than an epidemic. A pandemic is an infectious disease that is established across the world. Smallpox is an example of a pandemic. An endemic is an infectious disease present in certain areas or populations all of the time. It is often caused by an abnormality in plant or animal life exclusive to that area. Malaria, which is transported by the mosquito, is one example of an endemic. Through time, science has developed immunizations and medications to help fight some of these diseases and treat their symptoms. But for many, there is still no cure.

Write the topic of the paragraph on the line. Write the main idea in the top oval. Write three main supporting details in the next set of ovals. Write minor details in the rectangles.

Topic: _____

Comprehension: Informational Text

Read the text. Use the map on page 50 to outline how the major and minor details work together to support the main idea.

Vertebrates

Vertebrates are animals that have backbones. Animals without backbones are called invertebrates, or "not vertebrates." There are five different kinds of vertebrates: amphibians, birds, fish, mammals, and reptiles. Each type has distinct characteristics. Some are warm-blooded, while others are cold-blooded. Body coverings, habitats, reproduction, and methods of breathing differ from one to another. The one similarity that all vertebrates—no matter the shape or size—share is a skeletal structure with a backbone.

Amphibians are cold-blooded, skin-covered vertebrates. They have two distinct parts to their life cycle. The adult female lays jelly-like eggs that hatch into water creatures. Infant and juvenile amphibians have gills and spend their time in fluid environments. When they become adults, a transition is made and gills make way for lungs. Although many adult amphibians often need to stay moist, they must also breathe air. Frogs and salamanders are common examples of amphibians.

Like amphibians, birds can live around water. In fact, penguins are more comfortable in water than on land. Some of these feathered creatures, like kingfishers, even eat amphibians. Birds also live on nearly every type of land feature, and a majority spend much of their time airborne. Not all birds fly, but all birds are covered in feathers. Unlike amphibians, birds are warm-blooded. They breathe with lungs from the moment they hatch from brittle-shelled eggs. When first born, baby birds are helpless. Without parental care both while in the egg and after hatching, they would die.

Fish are lifelong water creatures. These cold-blooded animals are covered with scales and use gills to extract oxygen from the water. Most fish, like salmon, come from jelly-like eggs, but a few, such as guppies, develop inside the mother and are born alive. Fish generally do not care for their young. In fact, if a parent fish happens to come upon one of its offspring, the baby fish may become a snack.

Mammals are the only vertebrates whose females produce milk to feed their young. Nearly all mammals give birth to live young. They breathe with lungs and are warm-blooded, and most are covered with hair or fur. Because they are warm-blooded, mammals need to make their own heat, which requires additional energy and fuel in the form of food. Mammals have developed many ways to retain heat, such as thicker hair and fur in the winter months, layers of fat under the skin, and, in the case of humans, artificial coverings like clothing.

Comprehension: Informational Text

Although most mammals are land creatures, there is also a group of ocean-dwelling mammals. Many of these mammals are members of the whale family, such as orcas, porpoises, humpbacks, and dolphins. They live in a liquid environment and can hold their breath for long periods, but they, too, have lungs and must surface to breathe. Other types of mammals include seals, rats, kangaroos, tigers, elephants, dogs, and humans.

Reptiles are the final group of vertebrates. They are cold-blooded like amphibians and fish. They also lay eggs. Reptiles are covered with scales; some scales form shells like those of the turtle and tortoise groups. Reptiles lay leathery eggs. They also breathe with lungs. Turtles, alligators, and crocodiles spend much of their time in the water, but they are often found resting on logs or on shore, warming themselves in the midday sun.

Fill in the map. Write the main idea from the text in the top oval. Write the five major details from the text in the next set of ovals. Finally, write three minor details in the rectangles to support each of the five major details.

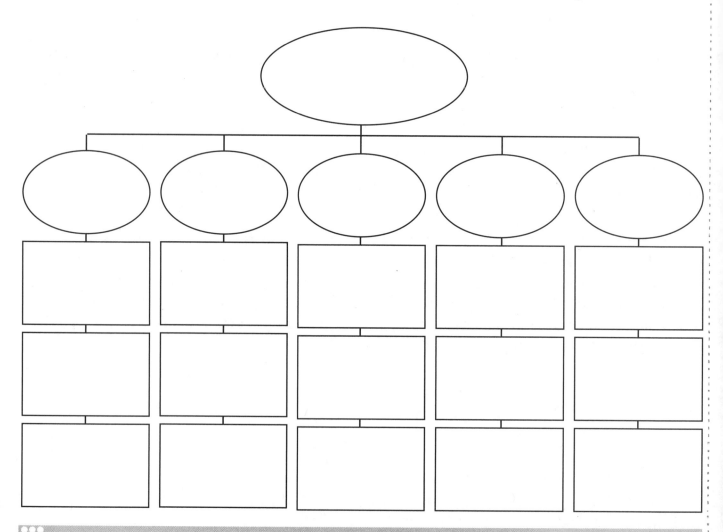

Comprehension: Informational Text

Read the passage. Then, answer the questions. Use information from the text to support your answers.

Microscopes

A microscope is a scientific tool that helps people to see very small things. By magnifying tiny objects many times, scientists can view intricate details. Hans and Zacharias Jenssen produced a tube with magnifying lenses at either end in the late 1500s. Anton van Leeuwenhoek developed a single-lens microscope in the mid-1600s. He was the first person to describe bacteria that he saw under the microscope. Early microscopes could magnify objects only up to 20 or 30 times their size, but Leeuwenhoek's device could magnify up to 200 times. Today, scientists use compound microscopes that have multiple lenses to further magnify an image up to 1,000 times. In 1931, two German scientists invented the electron microscope, which can magnify up to one million times. This device directs a beam of electrons at a cell sample to form an image that is captured on a photographic plate.

1. What is the main idea of this story?

   a. Scientists have developed and improved microscopes over time.

   b. Bacteria can be seen under a microscope.

   c. Compound microscopes use multiple lenses.

2. What did the device produced by Hans and Zacharias Jenssen look like?

   _____

3. What was Leeuwenhoek able to describe for the first time?

   _____

4. How has magnification in microscopes changed over time?

   _____

   _____

5. How does an electron microscope work?

   _____

   _____

Comprehension: Informational Text

Asthma

What do you know about asthma? Before you read the article, read each pair of statements. Write a **P** before the statement you predict is true based on your prior knowledge. Then read the article on the next two pages. Review your choices. Write a **V** in front of each verified answer. Write the number of the paragraph that contains the answer.

1. _____ a. Asthma is not contagious. It is a chronic lung condition.

   _____ b. Asthma is contagious. It is caused by a virus or bacteria.

   Answer found in paragraph _____

2. _____ a. Asthma can be cured.

   _____ b. Asthma can be controlled by taking medications and avoiding triggers.

   Answer found in paragraph _____

3. _____ a. Tight, mucus-filled bronchi won't let oxygen into the lungs.

   _____ b. Tight, mucus-filled bronchi trap carbon dioxide in the lungs.

   Answer found in paragraph _____

4. _____ a. All people with asthma have allergies.

   _____ b. Some people with allergies have asthma.

   Answer found in paragraph _____

5. _____ a. Anyone can develop asthma.

   _____ b. Asthmatics are born with asthma.

   Answer found in paragraph _____

6. _____ a. An asthmatic always has trouble breathing.

   _____ b. An asthmatic can have trouble breathing when a trigger is present.

   Answer found in paragraph _____

7. _____ a. All asthmatics have the same triggers.

   _____ b. Each asthmatic has different triggers.

   Answer found in paragraph _____

8. _____ a. Asthmatics can do all the things you do as long as they monitor their breathing.

   _____ b. Asthmatics can never run, exercise, or play sports.

   Answer found in paragraph _____

9. _____ a. Asthmatics go to the hospital each time they have trouble breathing.

   _____ b. Asthmatics can usually take care of their asthma from home, working with their doctors.

   Answer found in paragraph _____

Comprehension: Informational Text

Read the article. Then, answer the questions on page 54.

Asthma

You just found out your friend has asthma. All sorts of scary thoughts are going through your head: Can I catch it? Can my friend still do "normal" things? Is it safe to be around this person? Will my friend spend a lot of time indoors or in the hospital?

First of all, asthma is not contagious. You cannot catch it from someone else. It is not passed on by a bacteria or virus like the flu, strep throat, or a cold. A bacteria or virus can, however, trigger asthma symptoms in someone who already has asthma. Anyone can develop asthma, including children and adults. There is some evidence that the tendency to develop asthma may be hereditary, or passed on by parents, just like hair color or body size.

So, just what is asthma? Asthma is a chronic condition of one of the body's vital organs. These vital organs are the lungs. Asthma cannot be cured, but it can be managed with medications and by avoiding triggers. Asthma is an ongoing lung condition.

It helps to understand how the lungs work. Lungs are made up of bronchi, which are interconnecting passageways made to let oxygen and carbon dioxide pass between the body and the outside air. The bronchi branch off into smaller passageways called bronchioles. This entire system is often called the brachial tree. The bronchi are covered with cilia, which are small, hair-like projections that use mucus to sweep dust and other particles out of the lungs.

Asthma is a lung condition that acts differently with different people. But all asthmatics, or people with asthma, have oversensitive lungs. They have problems when the muscles surrounding the bronchi squeeze too tightly and the brachial tree produces too much mucus. This can make it hard for the asthmatic person to breathe and can also make her wheeze, or sound raspy when she breathes. Because the airways are tighter and contain extra mucus, carbon dioxide gets trapped in the lower parts of the brachial tree. It cannot get out, which results in a smaller area of the lungs being used for breathing. When oxygen is brought into the lungs, a smaller part is able to absorb it and bring it to the body. The problem is not taking in oxygen; it is the carbon dioxide trapped inside. The good news is that the lungs do not behave this way all of the time—only when a trigger is present.

When an asthma attack occurs, a trigger causes the airways to constrict, or get smaller, and produce more mucus, trapping carbon dioxide in the lungs. Triggers are different for each asthmatic and can include allergens, irritants, viruses or bacteria, exercise, or stress. Just because a person has an allergy does not mean he will have asthma, just as a person who has asthma does not necessarily have allergies.

Asthmatics can take care of their asthma at home if they work together with their doctors. An asthma attack does not have to mean a trip to the hospital. Many asthmatics have emergency medications and equipment at home: peak flow meters, inhalers, pills, and steroids. An acute attack occurs when an asthmatic cannot get his breathing under control. When this happens, a trip to the emergency room and a short stay in the hospital are necessary.

Asthmatics can lead "normal" lives. They can play sports, travel, and do all sorts of fun things. They do, however, need to be aware of their own triggers. Different things trigger asthma in different patients. It is not the same for everyone. Knowledge, the correct medications and equipment, and a good working relationship with a doctor are an asthmatic's best tools.

Comprehension: Informational Text

Answer the questions using information from the article on page 53.

1. What does the word "chronic" mean in paragraph 3? _____

_____

Highlight the answer with yellow.

2. What are bronchi? _____

_____

Highlight the answer with green.

3. How do bronchi affect an asthmatic? _____

_____

4. What is a trigger? _____

_____

Highlight the answer with blue.

5. List four possible triggers.

_____   _____

_____   _____

Comprehension: Informational Text

All living things proceed through a cycle of life. Each step allows the next to happen. The life cycle is continuous with enough of the species surviving each step to allow for the species to continue to live throughout time. Read the description of the plant life cycle. Use the information to complete the activities on pages 57 and 58.

Plant Life Cycle

The seed provides a safe haven for the defenseless baby plant. Each seed has three main parts: a seed coat, a cotyledon, and an embryo. The seed coat is the outer layer that surrounds the seed. It protects the seed from rough or extreme weather and from animal digestive tracts. The cotyledon, or stored food, takes up most of the space inside the seed. It will provide the germinating seed with the energy it needs to push through soil or other plant matter and provide the seedling with the nourishment it needs to begin to grow. The third part of the seed is the embryo. The embryo is the baby plant. It has an embryo root to push its way eventually out of the seed coat, an embryo stem, and embryo leaves which will later start food production.

SEED COAT →

EMBRYO

COTYLEDON

The seed will germinate, or begin to grow, when the time is right. It requires two things to germinate: water and warmth. Water is needed to soften the seed coat so that the embryo root can poke its way out of the seed and begin its descent into the soil. New roots grow quickly, helping to absorb even more water. As the embryo plant grows, the softened seed coat splits open. Warm temperatures are needed to sustain the young plant as it grows. Temperatures that are too cold will end the life cycle by killing the plant.

Once the young plant breaks through the soil, it is called a seedling. The seedling has three main parts: roots, a stem, and seed leaves. The seed leaves are often different in shape than the rest of the leaves that will later grow on the plant. The new seedling needs three things to survive. First, it needs water in the correct amount; too much causes drowning, and too little causes it to dry up. Second, the seedling needs warm temperatures, which will allow it to grow. Third, it needs food. The seedling begins with the stored food from the seed and will eventually make its own food as it grows into a larger plant.

Comprehension: Informational Text

As the seedling grows into a plant, many changes take place. The plant parts begin to perform their own specialized jobs. The roots grow down into the soil and hold the plant in the ground. They are the stabilizing force against wind, weather, and grazing animals. The roots also assist the plant by absorbing water and minerals from the soil. The leaves begin their kitchen job—they make and store food. Leaves use the water and minerals absorbed by the roots, carbon dioxide in the air, and sunlight to make food in their chlorophyll. This process uses the carbon dioxide produced by animals, automobiles, and factories to produce the oxygen needed by animals. The stem holds up the plant and becomes the distribution center, carrying water and minerals from the roots and produced food from the leaves to the parts of the plant that need them. These plants are found worldwide in many climates and physical conditions, from backyards to deserts to mountaintops to swamps. The list of locations is endless.

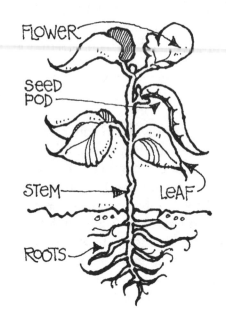

Seeds are produced in specialized parts of adult plants. Seeds can be produced in cones or flowers. Cones are produced in evergreen plants. Once they have been pollinated by wind, insects, or animals, flowers develop pods, fruits, or vegetables which house the new seeds. The seeds are then scattered to a new location where the cycle can continue. They can be scattered by animals, birds, wind, water, people, or gravity. Some seeds are eaten by animals or birds and pass through their digestive tracts in their waste. Other seeds, like burs, hitch a ride in fur, feathers, or socks. People also scatter seeds intentionally in gardens. The wind blows other seeds that are specially adapted to travel like small parachutes or umbrellas. Others float on freshwater streams or ocean currents to new locations. Spherical seeds use good old gravity to drop and roll. Each method of movement ensures enough space for the new generation to grow without crowding.

Then, when the time is right, a seed will begin to germinate, a seedling will grow, and the cycle will continue.

Comprehension: Informational Text

Use information from the article on pages 55 and 56 to answer the questions. Verify your answers by highlighting in the text where you found the information.

1. Where do seed plants grow? List six places. You may use two from the article.

   _____

2. What are some specific seed plants? List three. Example: a rose

   _____

3. What is the purpose of the seed coat? _____

4. What needs to happen before the plant embryo can push its way out of the seed coat?

   _____

5. What two things could stop the life cycle of an individual plant?

   _____

6. What are three ways that seeds can be scattered?

   _____

7. Using information from the text, define *germinate*.

   _____

8. What are the roots' two main jobs?

   _____

9. Where do seeds form? _____

10. What are the leaves' two main jobs?

   _____

Comprehension: Informational Text

Follow the directions to create a poster of the plant life cycle. Check off each step as you complete it.

Making a Poster of the Plant Life Cycle

_____ Write "Plant Life Cycle" in the center of the paper.

_____ Write your first and last names in the bottom right corner.

_____ Divide the paper into six sections. Label them in this order: seed parts, seed germination, seedling, seed plant, seed production, and seed scattering.

(In the appropriate sections:)

_____ Draw a seed. Show and label the three parts of the seed.

_____ Draw a germinating seed.

_____ Write the two things a seed needs in order to germinate.

_____ Draw and label a seedling. Include roots, stem, and seed leaves.

_____ List the three things a seedling needs in order to grow.

_____ Draw and label a plant. Include leaves, stem, and roots.

_____ Label the two jobs of a leaf.

_____ Include the three things a leaf needs in order to make food.

_____ Label the two jobs of the root system.

_____ Label the two jobs of a stem.

_____ Draw and list the two plant parts that produce seeds.

_____ List the three things a flower can make to house its seeds.

_____ List the six ways seeds are scattered.

_____ Draw a representation of one way seeds are scattered.

_____ Draw an arrow from each section to the next.

Comprehension: Informational Text

Read question 1 on page 60. Then, read the passage.

Making Our World a Better Place to Call Home

"Am I in school just to learn how to be an adult?" a sixth-grader once asked. "Do I have to wait for when I'm a grown-up before I'm a person? No. I'm a person now. Maybe I can't vote for our government, but I'm still a citizen in a family and a school and a community, and in our country and our world. This is our world too, not just the adults'!"

Many children have made a difference in the world. When the American colonies fought for independence, boys and girls as young as ten years old found ways to help. Some joined the army, and others spun wool for soldiers' uniforms. Children worked together to change child labor laws so that children could go to school instead of working sixty hours a week. Children were part of the Underground Railroad that helped slaves escape to freedom. And children helped in the struggle for civil rights for all citizens of the United States.

Today, many children are doing things to improve our world. In fact, as a child, you have advantages adults don't have when it comes to making changes happen.

Children are often idealistic. They have a clear sense of right and wrong. Adults often see issues as more complicated. Children often don't have to work full-time to support themselves or their families. They have more time to devote to other projects.

Children have a lot of energy, and they can draw attention to a project. Sometimes adults don't take kids seriously when they first start trying to make important changes in their communities. However, television and newspaper reporters usually love a story about children who are working for change. And when the story gets told in the media, adults take those children seriously.

Children already have a network of possible helpers. Kids who make changes often organize their efforts in their schools. They spread the word about a project through their classes, in the lunchroom, or on the playground. Sometimes they get advisors or sponsors, and they can take advantage of the school's other resources, such as photocopy machines or meeting rooms.

All of us want to make our world better. Even kids have the power to help make that happen.

Comprehension: Informational Text

Use the passage on page 59 to help you answer the questions.

1. Read only the title and the first sentence of each paragraph. Which of these sentences is closest to the main idea?

   a. We should clean up our environment.

   b. Kids don't have to wait to be adults to help make changes.

   c. Childhood is a time only for play, not for serious things.

   d. Children like drawing projects.

2. In which paragraph does the author introduce the idea of children influencing change? How does the author do this? Use information from the text to support your answer.

   _____

   _____

   _____

   _____

3. Complete each sentence with the correct word from the list.

   a. The charities worked together in a _____ .

   b. Television is one medium for news, and radio and newspapers are

      other _____ .

   c. He will be stronger if he will _____ himself to exercise.

   d. The _____ student tried to help the homeless man.

   idealistic

   devote

   media

   network

Comprehension: Informational Text

Read the passage. Then, answer the questions on page 62.

James Takes on Town Hall

One day, nine-year-old James Ale and his friend Bobby were playing catch in the street because they had nowhere else to play. Suddenly, a car sped around the corner and hit Bobby, breaking his leg.

James was angry that Bobby was hurt because he and his friends didn't have a safe place to play. He thought of the empty field behind the water plant. With playground equipment, a basketball court, and lights, it could be a safe park. He decided to make that park happen.

James got advice from his father and made a plan. He called the mayor and left a message. When she called back, James explained what had happened to Bobby and why the kids needed a park. The mayor said she would look into it. She called back again and explained that James's idea wouldn't work.

That's when James really went to work. He printed petitions and had kids sign them. Then he met with the mayor in person. When the mayor said there was no land available in his area, James pulled out his map on which he had marked the square of land behind the water plant. He also gave her the petition with the signatures. The mayor was impressed. A few weeks later, James met the mayor and town administrator at the site. The town administrator thought the site was too small.

James persisted. He called a reporter who wrote a story about James taking on town hall to get a park for the kids. James sent copies of the article to town officials. He kept calling the mayor to ask if there was any progress or if there was anything he could do to help.

Eventually James was invited to a town council meeting. In that meeting, the mayor announced the creation of a new park and asked James to stand and be recognized for helping to make the park happen.

Most people in Davie, Florida, now refer to that park as James Ale Park. It's the most popular playground in town. James Ale had a good idea, and he never gave up. He learned how to plan, how to organize, and how to lobby local government to make good things happen, even for kids.

Comprehension: Informational Text

Use the passage on page 61 to help you answer the questions.

1. How is the problem introduced in the passage?

_____

_____

2. Number the events in the order in which they happened.

_____ The new park is used by the kids.

_____ James lobbies town officials to build a park.

_____ James determines that the kids need a park.

_____ James's friend Bobby was hit by a car.

3. What is the main idea of the passage?

_____

_____

4. What did James do that helped him succeed?

_____

_____

_____

_____

_____

_____

Comprehension: Informational Text

Read the passage. Then, answer the questions on page 64.

Jason Builds a Library

Ten-year-old Jason Hardman loved to read, but the small rural town where he lived had no library. He decided to do something about that.

Jason went to the mayor and the town council. The mayor told him there was no money for a library, no place to put it, and no one to run it.

Jason shared his plan. The library could go in an empty room in the old rock schoolhouse. He would get people to donate books, and he would run the library. The council turned him down.

Jason didn't give up. He improved his plan and showed it to the mayor and town council again and again. Finally they agreed. He could use a room, but he wouldn't get any money or help. The room was a dingy mess, but Jason got his family and friends to help. They scrubbed the floor with wire brushes and cleaned the walls and ceiling. They added lights and built bookshelves. After hundreds of hours the room was ready.

Then Jason had to get books. He went door-to-door asking for books, and he called people in other towns. When he had 2,000 books, he opened the library.

Jason spent three hours each night running the library, but most of the time he was alone. People didn't use the library. He decided he didn't have the kinds of books people wanted to read. He wrote to publishers, politicians, and other libraries. Soon he was getting more books and more attention. A newspaper ran a story about Jason and his library. Other newspapers picked up Jason's story, and soon it was national news. Magazine writers and national talk shows interviewed the nation's youngest librarian. He testified at a congressional hearing on rural libraries. Soon publishers and people from across the country were donating books. With all the publicity and new books, more people used Jason's library. It grew so big that the town council that had rejected Jason started talking about a new building just for the library.

Within five years, the library Jason started had more than 17,000 books. Jason received awards from the governor of his state, the United States Library Commission, and even the president of the United States.

Comprehension: Informational Text

Use the passage on page 63 to help you answer the questions.

1. What is the main idea of the passage?

   _____

2. Based on this story, circle the words that describe Jason. Underline evidence in the passage.

   a. lazy

   b. persistent

   c. shy

   d. visionary (seeing what is possible)

3. Think like a reporter. Fill in the blanks with the correct details from the story.

   _____ (who) decided his

   _____ (where) needed a

   _____ (what).

   He _____ (how) the town council again and again, until they agreed.

   _____ (when) the room was ready. At first, people didn't use the

   library because _____ (why).

   He contacted publishers, politicians, and other libraries. Soon he got attention in the media, and he

   received thousands of books. The library became a success.

4. How is the problem introduced and developed in the passage?

   _____

   _____

   _____

   _____

   _____

   _____

Comprehension: Informational Text

Read question 1 on page 66. Then, read the passage.

Bullies

In the animal world, there are two reactions to bullies: fight or flight. But, you are a human being. You have more options than fight or flight. You have the ability to think and discuss your feelings with adults who can help you.

There are many ways to deal with bullies. First, think about how bullies tease or pick on people. They look for a victim and repeatedly tease the victim. Next, the victim becomes intimidated and the bully gains power. Bullies often behave this way because they are looking for a reaction. Often, bullying stems from emotions such as resentment, shame, and jealousy. Some people respond to bullies without thinking. They become angry, they obey the bully, or they become frightened. These reactions give the bully a sense of power. There are other ways to deal with bullies, such as being confident, finding support in your friends, and telling a trusted adult.

Luckily, there are many programs in place to help students deal with bullying. Over the years, many anti-bullying movements have taken place, including National Bullying Prevention Month and local movements put into place by schools and districts. Anti-bullying laws have also been put into place in many states.

As a result of bullying, some students deal with low self-esteem, depression, and feelings of loneliness. If you are being bullied or know someone that is being bullied, you should seek assistance from your teacher, school counselor, parent, or other trusted adult. You should know that you do not have to deal with bullying alone.

Comprehension: Informational Text

Use the passage on page 65 to help you answer the questions.

1. Read only the title and the first sentence of each paragraph. Which of these sentences is closest to the main idea?

   a. Bullies are really cowards.

   b. Fighting is the only way to stop a bully.

   c. Girls are never bullies or teasers.

   d. There are many techniques to stop bullies from teasing.

2. An idiom is a phrase that has a meaning different than what the words say exactly. Saying that someone is "all thumbs" means someone doesn't work well with his or her hands, not that someone has extra thumbs. Which of these phrases from the story are idioms?

   a. sense of power

   b. stop and think

   c. taking a detour

   d. push your buttons

3. To stop being a victim, a person must break the bullying cycle. Put these phrases that describe the bullying cycle in order.

   _____ The bully gains a sense of power.

   _____ The bully looks for a victim.

   _____ The victim gets angry or afraid.

   _____ The bully teases or intimidates.

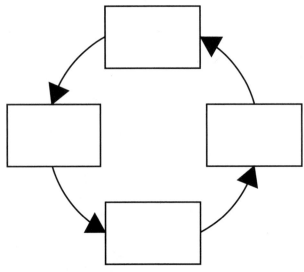

Comprehension: Informational Text

Read the passage. Then, answer the questions on page 68.

Making Friends

Friendship is a gift you give to others, as well as to yourself. A good friend doubles your joy and halves your burdens. Good friendships make life better by what you give and what you receive.

Sometimes friendship seems to just happen. But usually, building a good friendship takes patience and continued effort. So how do you make friends?

First, make yourself available for finding and making friends. Don't get so busy with your own activities that you don't get to know other people. Homework, reading, lessons, sports, and other activities are good. But even good activities can be overdone. Spending a lot of time watching television or playing video games by yourself can keep you from developing friendships.

Next, look for possible friends whenever you are with people. Consider the other kids in your classroom or the school cafeteria. Take a class in pottery, art, karate, or whatever interests you. Join a club. Attend summer camps. Volunteer at a nursing home or animal shelter. If you are involved in things you enjoy, chances are that other people there have interests and talents in common with you. They are good candidates for friends.

Don't wait for people to talk to you. Start a simple conversation. Most people are pleased if you show interest in them. If they don't respond, it's their loss. Be natural and don't worry about sounding dorky. You can discuss a class project, tell a joke, talk about a movie or the weather, ask for directions, or offer help. Once you get started, a conversation can take off on its own.

You probably know from experience that you can have many friends, but that only a few of those friends will become close friends. These friendships usually take a lot of time and effort to develop. They can start off just like other friendships, but eventually, as you talk and share experiences, some magic takes over. That's why it's important to get to know many people and put time and effort into developing friendships. You never know when one of those people will become your close and true friend.

Comprehension: Informational Text

Use the text on page 67 to help you answer the questions.

1. What is the main idea of the story?

   a. Pottery, art, and karate classes are fun.

   b. Making friends takes work, but it is worth it.

   c. Talking with people is easy.

   d. Not all of your friends will be your close friends.

2. Based on the passage, which of the following statements is a fact?

   a. You can never have too many friends.

   b. A good friend doubles your joy and halves your burdens.

   c. You can make new friends in the classroom or in the school cafeteria.

   d. People are pleased if you show interest in them.

3. Fill in this cluster with ideas from the story.

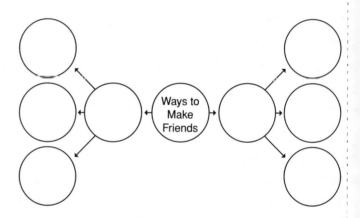

4. Using ideas from this story and your own ideas, make a list of things you can do to make friends.

_____

_____

5. What is a *candidate*?

_____

_____

Comprehension: Informational Text

Read question 1 on page 70. Then, read the passage.

Our Favorite Animal Teammate

Dogs have a reputation as man's best friend, but when it comes to sports, there is no animal we play with more than horses.

For as long as people have used horses for work, they have also used horses for play. Some ancient games, such as polo, are still popular today. Other ancient games, such as chariot racing, have been replaced by newer horse sports.

The modern rodeo grew out of horse and rider skills practiced by American cowboys in the Old West. In bareback and bronc riding, riders try to stay on bucking horses. Calf roping, steer roping, team roping, and steer wrestling all require athletic, well-trained horses. In barrel racing, cowgirls race their horses at breakneck speed in a cloverleaf pattern.

Gymkhanas are games British cavalry riders brought from India. In vaulting, a rider swings up to mount a horse that is already moving. In flag racing, a rider on a racing horse plants a flag in a small target on the ground.

Fox hunting has a long history in Europe and the United States. Lately, drag hunting has become a popular replacement. Instead of chasing a fox for miles, hounds chase an artificial scent that has been dragged over the hunt area, and the riders race after the hounds.

Endurance events are long-distance rides ranging from 25 to 100 or more miles. Some rides include orienteering, which means using a map and compass to find your way through a wilderness.

Polo is probably the best known team sport for horses and riders. However, new team games have also been invented. Polocrosse is similar to lacrosse on horseback. Horseball is like basketball played on horses. A ball with several handles is used. It has to be kept off the ground at all times. Riders try to take the ball from the other team and race to their end of a field to shoot the ball into a net for a score.

There are dozens of other events and games where horses and riders must work together. Show jumping, steeplechasing, flat racing, harness racing, and cross-country are just a few. But probably the most popular event will always be cooperative instead of competitive—riding just for pleasure.

Comprehension: Informational Text

Use the passage on page 69 to help you answer the questions.

1. Read only the title and the first paragraph. What can you infer about the rest of the story?

   a. The story is about people and horses together in sports.
   b. There are many different sports involving horses.
   c. All horse sports involve racing.
   d. The story is about different animals in sports.

2. Which paragraph tells about horse sports that were adapted from other sports?

   a. paragraph 3
   b. paragraph 4
   c. paragraph 5
   d. paragraph 7

3. Story Puzzle

   Across
   2. open-country obstacle course
   5. extremely fast
   6. odor
   8. known for something
   10. sport of cowboys
   11. two-wheeled cart

   Down
   1. horse mounting
   3. map and compass work
   4. perseverance
   7. best-known horse sport
   9. herds cattle

4. What is the main idea of this passage?

   _____

   _____

Comprehension: Informational Text

Read the passage. Then, answer the questions. Use information from the text to support your answers.

Becoming a Canadian Citizen

Until 1947, people living in Canada were considered citizens of Great Britain. That year, the Canadian government passed a Citizenship Act declaring that its people were Canadian citizens. For the first time, they were able to use Canadian passports rather than British passports. Today, about 150,000 people become Canadian citizens every year. First, they must become permanent residents. This is a special legal status that says that a person has been approved to live permanently in Canada. After three years, a permanent resident is eligible to apply for Canadian citizenship. The person must be able to speak either English or French and must not have committed a crime in the past three years. The person must also pass a citizenship test to show that he or she knows Canadian history, geography, and government. After passing the test, new citizens take an oath during a citizenship ceremony declaring their allegiance to the British monarch and to Canada.

1. What is the main idea of this story?

    a. Canadians used to be British citizens.

    b. Many immigrants move to Canada each year.

    c. People who want to become Canadian citizens must complete several steps.

2. What did the Citizenship Act of 1947 declare?

    _____

    _____

3. Define permanent *resident*. _____

    _____

4. What does it mean to become a permanent resident of Canada?

    _____

    _____

5. What do citizens state when taking the oath of citizenship?

    _____

Comprehension: Informational Text

Read the passage. Then, answer the questions. Use information from the text to support your answers.

Languages of Canada

Canada has two official languages: English and French. Because the Constitution lists these languages as official, all federal laws must be printed in both languages. Many other languages are also spoken in Canada, including Chinese, Spanish, and Arabic. There are also over 50 Aboriginal languages, or languages spoken by natives. One or two languages are more common in different provinces or geographical regions. In some more populous provinces, such as Ontario and British Columbia, a greater variety of languages are spoken. This may be because more immigrants from other countries live in these areas and bring their native languages to Canada. Each province may choose whether to designate an official provincial language. The official language of Quebec is French. It is the primary language for over 80 percent of the people who live there. A majority of the people in the province of Nunavut speak an Inuit language.

1. What is the main idea of this story?

   a. Most people in Canada speak either English or French.

   b. Over 50 Aboriginal languages are spoken in Canada.

   c. Canada has two official languages, but many others are also spoken in Canada.

2. Why must all Canadian federal laws be printed in both English and French?

   _____

   _____

3. What are Aboriginal languages?

   a. languages spoken by native peoples

   b. languages spoken only in Nunavut

   c. languages that are not written down

4. Why might more languages be spoken in some provinces than in others?

   _____

   _____

5. What is the official provincial language in Quebec?

   _____

Comprehension: Informational Text

Read the passage. Then, answer the questions. Use information from the text to support your answers.

Languages of the United States

Although most people in the United States speak English, the country does not have an official language. English is used for official documents, laws, and court decisions. However, some areas require publications to be printed in another language if there are many speakers of that language living there. Thirty states have adopted English as their official language. Only one state, Hawaii, is officially bilingual. This means that the state recognizes two official languages, English and Hawaiian. Many people in the U.S. states bordering Mexico speak both English and Spanish. Other states, such as Louisiana and Maine, have a large number of French speakers. Many Native American languages are spoken on reservations, areas of land managed by native groups such as the Navajo and the Seminole. Because the United States is a nation of many immigrants, some people are reluctant to declare only one official language.

1. What is the main idea of this story?

   a. The United States has no official language, but many languages are spoken in the United States.

   b. Most people in the United States speak English.

   c. Spanish and French are spoken in some U.S. states.

2. What are some official publications for which English is used?

   _____

3. When might a publication need to be printed in another language?

   _____

   _____

4. Which two states have a large number of French speakers?

   _____

5. What is a reservation?

   _____

   _____

Comprehension: Compare/Contrast

Read two campers' descriptions of waking up on Frog Pond. Then, answer the questions.

Camping on Frog Pond

Camper One   We woke this morning to waves lapping the shore, a breeze rustling the leaves, and the sounds of sweet baby frogs cricking to each other. They woke the swans and ducks who sang good morning to the animals around the pond. Soon every insect, bird, and animal was calling good morning to each other. How could I stay in bed? I needed to greet the morning, too.

Camper Two   We woke this morning to the incessant sound of frogs in the pond. Their shrill alarm triggered off-key honking and quacking from around the pond. The waves slapped the shore while the wind sandpapered everything in its path. Within 60 seconds, every insect, bird, and animal seemed to be protesting the hour. With this cacophony continuing, it was hardly worth going back to sleep.

1. How does Camper One feel about waking up on Frog Pond?

_____

Highlight word choices that support your answer.

2. How does Camper Two feel about waking up on Frog Pond?

_____

Highlight word choices that support your answer.

3. After reading both pieces, state four facts about what happened at Frog Pond that morning. Do not include any opinion words.

_____

_____

_____

4. What is the main idea of each passage? _____

5. How does each author present his or her view of the pond? _____

_____

_____

Comprehension: Compare/Contrast

Read the two passages on pages 75 and 76 about making change happen. As you read, think about how the two authors present the topic of change.

Organizing to Make Change Happen

What do you see that needs changing? Is it something in your neighborhood? Or is it something much bigger? Whatever it is, by using some imagination and having faith in yourself, you can make a difference. Perhaps your efforts will help only one person. That's great. But maybe your efforts will benefit a whole community of living things: plants, animals, or human beings.

One person can make a difference. However, usually a group of people can make a bigger difference. If you feel strongly about an issue, there are probably other kids who feel the same way. Organize a group to work on the problem.

Group work will be more effective if you do four things: (1) Write a mission statement that defines exactly what you want to accomplish. (2) Schedule regular meetings. (3) Give each person a responsibility. (4) Make the work fun!

Adult advisors can help. They have more access to resources. Make certain to choose adults who will help but who will not try to take over.

Knowledge is power. The more you know about your cause, the better. Make a long list of questions. What is the real problem? Who is responsible? What laws apply? How much money would it take to make a change?

Then research answers to your questions. The Internet can be a good place to start, but don't overlook your public library. Many libraries have staff that can help you find answers. Also, develop your own information. Gather statistics by observation and interviews. Try to understand all sides of the issue.

Once you understand all sides of the issue, if you still feel strongly about the need for change, develop a plan of action. Your goal is the heart of your plan. Break down your goal into smaller objectives. Then make assignments. Each objective should have a person who is responsible for it and a deadline. Finally, do the work you need to do to make sure your plan stays on schedule.

With passion for change, knowledge, the help of others, and a plan, you are on your way to making a difference in the world.

Comprehension: Compare/Contrast

Tools for Making Change Happen

If you want to bring about positive change in your world, you need to take action. Here are some of the tools you can use.

Use Petitions. A petition states the problem and the changes you propose. It includes signatures of people who agree with you. Petitions show decision makers and the media how many people want the change.

Use the Media. Newspaper and television reporters need interesting stories for their readers and viewers. Contact reporters who cover your issue and show them why your story is interesting.

Build a Website. Organize your research on the problem. Create a website about the problem and the changes that should be made. Use keywords about the issue in your titles so search engines can find you.

Send Letters, Postcards, and Emails. Use letters, postcards, and emails to explain the problem, propose changes, ask for support, or thank people. Target people who should be interested. Be respectful.

Speak to Groups. If you are concerned about a local issue, the town meeting is a good place to be heard. Your comments will become part of the public record. Clubs and other organizations also look for good speakers.

Work with Elected Officials. Officials are elected to make things better for their community. Find an official who is interested in your issue. Then work together to solve the problem.

Negotiate. If you are trying to get an organization to change, you may need to negotiate. Know exactly what you want changed, but also know what smaller changes would be good for now.

Boycott. To boycott is to not buy products from a company you think is doing something wrong. Make sure your facts are correct. Then get as many people as possible to join the boycott. It can be a powerful tool for change.

Demonstrate and Protest. If your other tools aren't working, or if the problem is urgent, you may consider demonstrating: marching, picketing, and carrying signs. Be creative if you want to draw attention to the issue and help educate and influence people. Also, be aware of any laws about demonstrations or meetings that you will need to obey. Make sure what you are doing does not cause harm.

Sometimes kids see problems adults overlook. Kids can gain real power to make good changes when they organize and use the right tools to get their message out.

Comprehension: Compare/Contrast

Use the passage on page 75 to answer the questions.

1. Based on this story, which of these statements are true?

   a. Only a group of people can make change happen.

   b. A person has to understand all sides of an issue before acting.

   c. Our world improves as people work to improve it.

   d. Only adults should be the leaders of groups working for change.

2. Based on paragraph seven, which of these statements are true?

   a. A goal is the one main objective.

   b. A goal can be broken down into smaller parts or objectives.

   c. A good leader does all of the work alone.

   d. A plan of action should include deadlines and a schedule.

3. What is an *objective*?

   _____

4. Make a list of things you see that should be improved in your area or in our world.

   _____

   _____

   _____

   _____

5. What is the main idea of this passage?

   _____

   _____

   _____

Comprehension: Compare/Contrast

Use the passage on page 76 to answer the questions.

1. Based on this story, which of these statements are true?

   a. Letters and emails can be used to gather financial support for a cause.

   b. Being obnoxious is the best way to get support for a cause.

   c. Kids can help improve our world.

   d. Kids can never be speakers in town meetings.

2. Match the cause on the left with its main effect on the right.

   _____ A large group boycotts a product.

   _____ A person has petitions signed.

   _____ A small group demonstrates in a busy public area.

   _____ A person works with an elected official on a legal issue.

   > 1. A bill is introduced to change a law.
   > 2. People become aware of the issue.
   > 3. Decision makers know that many people are interested in the issue.
   > 4. The company loses sales.

3. What is the main idea of this passage?

   _____

   _____

4. Reread the passages on pages 75 and 76. Compare and contrast how each author presents the topic of change. How are the passages similar? How are they different?

   _____

   _____

   _____

   _____

   _____

   _____

Comprehension: Compare/Contrast

Read the passages on pages 79 and 80. Then, answer the questions. Use information from the text to support your answers.

Exploring Space

People have been fascinated by outer space for centuries. The first animals sent into space were fruit flies, which traveled on a U.S. rocket in 1947. Many countries sent monkeys into space to investigate how space travel might affect humans. A Russian dog named Laika became the first animal to orbit Earth in 1957. In 1961, the Russian cosmonaut Yuri Gagarin became the first person to travel into space. His spacecraft orbited Earth once and then landed. In 1969, the American astronaut Neil Armstrong became the first person to walk on the moon. The United States developed a space shuttle during the 1980s that could be used many times, like an airplane. Russia built a space station called Mir that was used for many years. Astronauts began assembling the International Space Station in 1998. This research station is a cooperative project among many countries, including the United States, Russia, Japan, Brazil, Canada, and 11 European countries.

1. What is the main idea of this story?

    a. People have always been fascinated by outer space.

    b. Space travel has improved greatly over the past several decades.

    c. Mir was a Russian space station.

2. Why did many countries send monkeys into space?

    _____

3. Who was the first person to travel into space?

    _____

4. What was significant about the space shuttle?

    _____

5. What is the International Space Station?

    _____

    _____

Comprehension: Compare/Contrast

Read the text. Then, answer the questions.

Moon Beverage

Space travel has long captured the human imagination. Rocket into space and explore the star-infested darkness! Drop down on Mars, perhaps Jupiter and Saturn! Ready to take off? Sorry, it is currently impossible. Problems include finding ways to transport oxygen for breathing and fuel for traveling. But the Moon and a frozen earth beverage may soon help solve some of these problems.

In 1998, NASA launched the Lunar Prospector on a 19-month mission. This spacecraft's job was to map and explore the Moon from orbit, then make a controlled landing on the Moon's south pole. It had many specialized instruments onboard to assist with its mission. One instrument, called the neutron spectrometer, was designed to detect minute amounts of water ice. In 1998, the Lunar Prospector collected information indicating the likelihood of solid water existing on the Moon.

The mission determined that frozen pockets of water are most likely located in many of the Moon's craters. These deep craters have areas that are in bitterly frigid constant darkness. These craters, well below 0°F, are definitely cold enough to freeze and keep frozen water, which freezes at just 32°F.

What makes water such a precious beverage? It is made up of two hydrogen molecules and one oxygen molecule. The water on the Moon could be separated and used to provide oxygen for breathing and hydrogen for fuel. Where could this water have come from? No one is certain, but many scientists believe it came from space debris that has bombarded the Moon over time. Is a manned station planned for any time soon? Information will need to be studied, hypotheses confirmed, then . . . possibly.

1. What problems currently stop space travel? _____

2. Highlight three facts about the Lunar Prospector stated in the text. _____

3. What is a neutron spectrometer? _____

4. What were the Lunar Prospector's findings regarding frozen water? _____

_____

5. Why is finding water important? _____

6. If there is water on the Moon, how did it get there? _____

7. On another sheet of paper, compare and contrast how each author presents the topic of space travel. How are the passages similar? How are they different?

Comprehension: Integrating Knowledge

Bicycle Safety

Faiza presented a report on bicycle safety to her class. She polled her classmates about their own bicycle safety before and after her presentation. She then compiled the two frequency tables below. In her report, Faiza included safety rules and read statistics on bicycle-related injuries and deaths each year. She also pointed out that one of the most critical safety issues was wearing a helmet every time you ride a bicycle.

Safety before Report	Yes	No
Do you think you will always check your brakes, seat, handlebars, and tires before riding?	1	24
Do you think you will always wear a helmet?	9	16
Do you think you will always pay attention to all traffic signs?	12	13
Do you think you will regularly ride on the handlebars or with two people on a bike?	10	15
Do you think you will always walk your bike across busy intersections?	3	22

Prediction after Report	Yes	No
Do you think you will always check your brakes, seat, handlebars, and tires before riding?	16	9
Do you think you will always wear a helmet?	22	3
Do you think you will always pay attention to all traffic signs?	22	3
Do you think you will regularly ride on the handlebars or with two people on a bike?	2	23
Do you think you will always walk your bike across busy intersections?	22	3

Use the information above to answer the following questions.

1. Compare both sets of data. Write two true, specific statements comparing them. Use information from the

   text to support your answer. _____

   _____

2. Based on the data, what conclusion could Faiza make about her report?

   a. Her report influenced her classmates.

   b. Her report was about safety.

   c. Her report did not get a passing grade.

3. Which details in Faiza's report may have caused the post-report results?

   _____

   _____

Comprehension: Integrating Knowledge

Read the passage. Then, answer the questions on page 83.

Great Lakes

The Great Lakes, located in North America, are the largest bodies of fresh water in the world. It is generally believed that they were made by glaciers that once covered the area. As the glaciers retreated, they gouged and filled the five Great Lakes as well as many other smaller lakes and rivers in the area.

Today, the Great Lakes are shared by two countries: the United States and Canada. The lakes provide people in the area with fresh water for drinking and for use in the home. They also assist many power plants and manufacturing companies. Recreation and transportation are two additional benefits. These lakes are also home to numerous freshwater fish like salmon, perch, trout, and walleye.

Lake Superior is the deepest of the five lakes. It also lies the farthest north. This lake is cold year-round and can develop violent storms. Because of this, many ships lie at the bottom of Lake Superior, including the famous *Edmund Fitzgerald*. The Soo Locks, completed in 1855, connect Lake Superior to Lake Huron, which is over 20 feet lower. The locks were built to transport large ships and goods. Lake Superior is the largest freshwater lake in the world.

Lake Huron is named for an Indian tribe that once lived along its shores. This lake has more islands than any of the other four Great Lakes. Most of these islands are nearer to the Canadian border than the Michigan border. Lake Huron touches Lake Superior at the Soo Locks, Lake Michigan at the Straits of Mackinac, and Lake Erie to the south.

Lake Michigan is the only Great Lake located entirely within the United States. The rest share boundaries with Canada and the U.S. Lake Michigan borders Wisconsin, Illinois, Indiana, and Michigan.

Lake Erie reaches the farthest south of any of the Great Lakes. It is also the shallowest. The most eastern Great Lake is Lake Ontario.

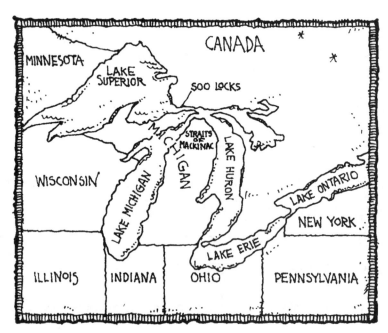

Comprehension: Integrating Knowledge

Use the passage on page 82 to answer the questions.

1. How were the Great Lakes formed?

_____

_____

2. How are the Great Lakes used by the people living on their borders?

_____

_____

Use the clues below and information in the text and map to assist you in completing the problem-solving matrix below.

- The deepest Great Lake is also the largest.
- A lake that connects at the Straits of Mackinac has the second largest area.
- The shallowest lake is not the smallest in area.
- The lake without a Canadian border has the third largest area.

		Area (in square miles)				
		7,320	9,910	22,300	23,000	31,700
Great Lakes	Erie					
	Huron					
	Michigan					
	Ontario					
	Superior					

Lake Erie covers _____ square miles.

Lake Huron covers _____ square miles.

Lake Michigan covers _____ square miles.

Lake Ontario covers _____ square miles.

Lake Superior covers _____ square miles.

Comprehension: Integrating Knowledge

Read the passage and the table. Then, answer the questions on pages 84 and 85.

Sleep Tight

Getting enough sleep is extremely important. This is the time the heart, lungs, muscles, nervous system, digestive system, and skeletal system get a chance to rest and get ready for another busy day. Insufficient sleep results in a sleep debt, or an amount of sleep owed your body. Sleep debt definitely affects the way a person functions. People with this deficit may not think they are sleepy, but they are less able to concentrate. They are also irritable and emotional and may have trouble reacting. In fact, some people with a sleep debt can act in ways that mimic the symptoms of attention deficit disorder (ADD). Uninterrupted sleep in which the sleeper reaches and maintains REM, or rapid eye movement, sleep is the key. It is in this stage of sleep that the body and brain get the relief needed in order to function at their optimum levels the next day. Every individual has his own sleep needs, but researchers have determined the approximate amount of sleep needed by school-age children. These times do not include time spent reading in bed, talking, or thinking about the next day. Add to the times below the amount of time it takes you to fall asleep.

Amount of sleep needed by school-age children	
Age	Suggested hours of uninterrupted sleep
1–6 years old	10–12 hours
6–12 years old	9–11 hours
12–18 years old	8–10 hours

1. According to this table, if an 11-year-old gets up at 6:30 a.m., what is the latest time she should fall asleep?

_____

2. What is a "sleep debt"? _____

3. Why is sleep so important? _____

_____

4. What happens to a person who does not get enough sleep? Name two effects.

_____

_____

5. What type of sleep is the most important for your body? _____

Comprehension: Integrating Knowledge

6. According to the table, how much sleep should you get each night? _____

_____

7. What time do you get up in the morning? _____

   What is the latest you should fall asleep each night? _____

8. If you were to get the greatest amount of recommended sleep,

   what time would you fall asleep? _____

9. What time did you go to sleep last night? _____

   According to the table, did you get enough sleep? _____

Use the graph to record the amount of sleep you get over the course of one week. List the days across the bottom. Begin with the number of hours you slept last night.

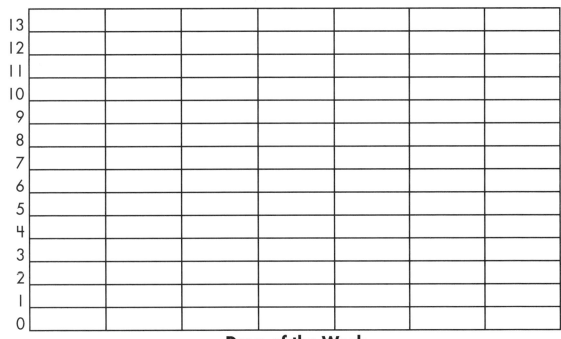

Evaluate your graph. Write two true statements based upon the data you collected.

_____

Context Clues

Read the sentences below. Choose the word in the word box that is a synonym, or word with nearly the same meaning, for the boldfaced word. Then, write it on the line below the sentence.

considered	told	increase	threatened	critical
document	billfold	collecting	empty	

1. The storyteller **narrated** the tale in a deep, booming voice.

   _____

2. I received a **certificate** that said I had successfully completed the course.

   _____

3. The mayor said that providing funding for the hospital was an **urgent** issue.

   _____

4. The judge **contemplated** the evidence before making her decision.

   _____

5. That house has been **vacant** for several months.

   _____

6. Dad took a $10 bill out of his **wallet** and handed it to the clerk.

   _____

7. The habitat of many animals is **endangered**.

   _____

8. My uncle has been **accumulating** baseball cards since he was a child.

   _____

9. The large speakers **amplify** the volume of the music.

   _____

Context Clues

Read the sentences below. Choose the word in the word box that is a synonym for the boldfaced word. Then, write it on the line below the sentence.

> bendable   achieve   quick   greatest   bright
> cautiously   feed   hobby   forceful

1. Grandpa likes to wear shirts with **vivid** colors when he plays golf.

   _____

2. The children's toy is made out of **flexible** plastic.

   _____

3. My favorite **pastime** is painting pictures of flowers using watercolors.

   _____

4. Mom **gingerly** opened the door to find out where the noise was coming from.

   _____

5. If you work hard, you can **attain** any goal.

   _____

6. The announcer told us in an **emphatic** voice that the train was about to depart.

   _____

7. The **maximum** number of students in a class at my sister's school is 22.

   _____

8. It is important to **nourish** your body with healthy foods.

   _____

9. Cherie walked across the room with a **brisk** stride.

   _____

Context Clues

Read the sentences below. Choose the word in the word box that is a synonym, or word with nearly the same meaning, for the boldfaced word. Then, write it on the line below the sentence.

peaceful	spines	nimble	slight	eagerness
beautiful	certain	confused	exact	

1. The weather forecaster said that there was only a **scant** chance of rain.

   _____

2. I was **perplexed** by the math problem at first, but then it began to make sense.

   _____

3. The pond was very **tranquil** at sunset.

   _____

4. Rita's gold necklace is **exquisite**.

   _____

5. We were asked to give a **literal** translation of the Spanish phrase.

   _____

6. A hedgehog's **bristles** help protect it from predators.

   _____

7. Our coach felt **confident** that we could win the game.

   _____

8. The gymnast was very **agile** on the balance beam.

   _____

9. Abel has a great **fervor** for learning and spends every Saturday at the library.

   _____

Context Clues

Read the sentences below. Use the context clues to figure out the definition of each boldfaced word. Then, write the letter of the correct definition on the line.

a. showed how

b. people who move from another country

c. decision

d. made shorter

e. plans

f. able to be changed

g. provide nutrients

h. usually

i. mechanical device

j. forecasted

1. The word *doctor* can be **abbreviated** as *Dr.* _____

2. Ms. Yang **demonstrated** how to complete the experiment. _____

3. My brother and I **typically** spend each summer at our grandmother's house. _____

4. The sportscaster **predicted** that the visiting team would win the game. _____

5. My **schedule** includes activities every day after school. _____

6. The coach asked us to keep our plans **flexible** in case our team made the playoffs. _____

7. Eating a variety of foods helps to **nourish** the body. _____

8. My mother's parents were **immigrants** from Russia. _____

9. Mom fixed the **mechanism** so that she could move the garage door up and down. _____

10. The judge said that she had reached a **verdict**. _____

Context Clues

Read the sentences below. Use the context clues to figure out the definition of each boldfaced word. Then, write the letter of the correct definition on the line.

a. a part played by an actor

b. at the edge

c. common saying

d. left out

e. characteristics of a surface

f. satisfied

g. at the same time

h. pull out

i. took back

j. stages

1. My uncle used a hammer to **wrench** the nail out of the board. _____

2. Daniel tried out for a **role** in the school play. _____

3. Silk has a very smooth **texture**. _____

4. Our class called out the answer to the question in **unison**. _____

5. I **retrieved** my hat from the lost-and-found box. _____

6. We learned about the **phases** of the moon in science class. _____

7. Tony **quenched** his thirst after the race by drinking water. _____

8. The scientists believed that they were on the **verge** of finding a cure for the disease. _____

9. An old **maxim** is "A stitch in time saves nine." _____

10. The teacher accidentally **omitted** Cathy's name from the list. _____

Name

Context Clues

Read the sentences below. Use the context clues to figure out the definition of each boldfaced word. Then, write the letter of the correct definition on the line.

a. put forward

b. not well-known

c. manner of walking

d. wool

e. book about a person's life

f. pushed by bumping

g. in part

h. to begin or start

i. noticed

j. figured out

1. Our assignment is to write a summary of a **biography**. _____

2. Mia **asserted** her opinion at the meeting. _____

3. Please take your seats because the presentation is about to **commence**. _____

4. We **deduced** the answer to the problem. _____

5. The topic of her report is an **obscure** painter from the Middle Ages. _____

6. My project is only **partially** complete. _____

7. Amanda has a very fast **gait**, so it is hard to keep up with her. _____

8. My arm was **jostled** when someone tried to move past me in the crowd. _____

9. The science teacher asked us to write everything we **perceived**. _____

10. The sheep's **fleece** was thick. _____

Greek and Latin Roots

Many English words contain roots from other languages such as Greek and Latin. For example, the word *monarch* contains the roots *mon*, meaning "one," and *arch*, meaning "ruler." Therefore, a *monarch* is "one ruler," or a person who rules a country alone. Read the list of roots below.

bio: life	**ast:** star	**zoo:** animals	**geo:** earth
psych: mind	**archaeo:** ancient	**bot:** plant	**anthrop:** human

Use these roots to help you match the following words with their meanings.

archaeologist	zoologist	psychologist	biologist
anthropologist	botanist	astronomer	geologist

1. scientist who studies plants _____

2. scientist who studies the human mind _____

3. scientist who studies ancient people _____

4. scientist who studies different life forms _____

5. scientist who studies the earth _____

6. scientist who studies human cultures _____

7. scientist who studies the solar system _____

8. scientist who studies animals _____

Greek and Latin Roots

Many English words contain roots from other languages such as Greek and Latin. For example, the word *thermometer* contains the roots *therm* and *meter*. *Therm* means "heat," and *meter* means "to measure." Therefore, a *thermometer* is a device that measures heat. Read the list of roots below.

> **dent:** tooth   **cardi:** heart   **neur:** nerve   **pod:** foot
>
> **hemo:** blood   **ped:** child   **opt:** eye   **derm:** skin

Use these roots to match the following words with their meanings. Write the correct word in each blank.

> cardiologist   hematologist   dermatologist   pediatrician
>
> ophthalmologist   neurologist   podiatrist   dentist

1. doctor who examines blood _____

2. doctor who examines feet _____

3. doctor who examines children _____

4. doctor who examines teeth _____

5. doctor who examines the nervous system _____

6. doctor who examines skin _____

7. doctor who examines the heart _____

8. doctor who examines eyes _____

Greek and Latin Roots

Many English words contain roots from other languages such as Greek and Latin. For example, the word *bicycle* contains the roots *bi* and *cycl*. *Bi* means "two," and *cycl* means "a circle or ring." Therefore, a *bicycle* is a vehicle that has two circles, or wheels. Read the list of roots below.

omni: all	**nutri:** nourish	**herba:** grass	**spir:** breathe
phys: body, nature	**carn:** meat	**aero:** air	**chlor:** green

Use these roots to help you match the following words with their meanings.

herbivore	nutrition	physical	respiration
aerobic	carnivore	chlorophyll	omnivore

1. something that makes plants' leaves green _____

2. animal that eats only plants _____

3. taking in the food necessary for health and growth _____

4. the act of breathing _____

5. animal that eats only meat _____

6. helping the body take in more oxygen _____

7. relating to the body _____

8. animal that eats all kinds of food _____

Greek and Latin Roots

Many English words contain roots from other languages such as Greek and Latin. For example, the word *submarine* contains the roots *sub* and *marine*. *Sub* means "below," and *marine* means "water." Therefore, a *submarine* is a vehicle that travels below the water. Read the list of roots below.

ann: year	**auto:** self	**loc:** place	**chron:** time
dem: people	**fac:** make	**spec:** see	**biblio:** book

Use these roots to match the following words with their meanings.

democracy   bibliography   location   chronology

factory   spectator   anniversary   autobiography

1. place where things are made _____

2. position of something _____

3. date marking a yearly event _____

4. person who watches something _____

5. list of events in order _____

6. book about a person's own life _____

7. government by the people _____

8. list of reference books _____

Greek and Latin Roots

Many English words contain roots from other languages such as Greek and Latin. For example, the word *television* contains the roots *tele* and *vision*. *Tele* means "distance," and *vision* means "to see." Therefore, a *television* is an object that lets you see things from a distance. Read the list of roots below.

cred: believe	**jud:** law	**crypt:** hidden	**temp:** time
mar: sea	**leg:** read	**aud:** hear	**port:** carry

Use these roots to match the following words with their meanings.

audible	temporary	credible	marine
cryptic	judicial	legible	portable

1. able to be carried _____

2. relating to the law _____

3. relating to the sea _____

4. able to be believed _____

5. lasting for only a short time _____

6. able to be read _____

7. mysterious _____

8. able to be heard _____

Greek and Latin Roots

Many English words contain roots from other languages such as Greek and Latin. For example, the word *monorail* contains the roots *mono* and *rail*. *Mono* means "one," so a *monorail* is a vehicle that runs on a single rail. Read the list of roots below.

cap: take, seize	**brev:** short	**ver:** truth	**magn:** large
nomen: name	**alter:** other	**nov:** new	**cogn:** know

Use these roots to match the following words with their meanings.

alternate	recognize	abbreviate	magnify
novice	nominate	verify	captivate

1. to be familiar with _____

2. to make larger _____

3. to hold someone's attention _____

4. to make shorter _____

5. to change between two things _____

6. to make sure something is true _____

7. to name someone as a candidate for office _____

8. someone who is new at doing something _____

Decoding Using Word Parts

Compound words are two words that have been joined to form another word. They do not always keep the meanings of both words. For example, a *skyscraper* does not actually scrape the sky. A *skyscraper* is a very tall building. In the chart below, write the literal meaning for each word that makes up the compound word. Then, write what the compound word means.

Compound Word	Literal Meaning for First Word	Literal Meaning for Second Word	Actual Meaning
1. airport			
2. jellyfish			
3. newspaper			
4. upstairs			
5. playground			
6. bookkeeper			
7. waterfall			
8. birthday			
9. popcorn			
10. afternoon			

Decoding Using Word Parts

Compound words are two words that have been joined to form another word. They do not always keep the meanings of both words. For example, a *brainstorm* does not actually mean "a storm occurring in the brain." A *brainstorm* is when you think of a lot of ideas for solving a problem. In the chart below, write the literal meaning for each word that makes up the compound word. Then, write what the compound word means.

Compound Word	Literal Meaning for First Word	Literal Meaning for Second Word	Actual Meaning
1. uproot			
2. airplane			
3. whirlpool			
4. shortstop			
5. haircut			
6. clothespin			
7. postcard			
8. supermarket			
9. teacup			
10. sailboat			

Decoding Using Word Parts

Portmanteau words were made by combining two words. For example, the word brunch was made by combining breakfast and lunch. Make a new word by combining the words in each row to make a word in the word box. Then, write what the new word means.

Internet	flare	moped	glimmer	motel	smog
motorcade	crunch	splatter	spork	fanzine	sitcom

1. flame + glare = _____ meaning: _____

2. smoke + fog = _____ meaning: _____

3. motorcar + parade = _____ meaning: _____

4. crispy + munch = _____ meaning: _____

5. motor + hotel = _____ meaning: _____

6. spoon + fork = _____ meaning: _____

7. gleam + shimmer = _____ meaning: _____

8. splash + spatter = _____ meaning: _____

9. international + network = _____ meaning: _____

_____

10. fan + magazine = _____ meaning: _____

11. motor + pedal = _____ meaning: _____

12. situation + comedy = _____ meaning: _____

Figurative Language

Read the poem. Then complete the activities.

Winter Sunrise
by J. P. Wallaker

Rose fingernails push back
star-sparkled blanket.

Warm toes slide out,
feel cold morning.

Pink pajama-clad body sits on side of bed,
shivering,
standing,
stretching.

Sparkle . . .
A snow day.

1. To what does this poem compare a sunrise? _____

2. Think of a sunrise. Make connections between the poem and an actual sunrise. Write a literal interpretation for each image.

Fingernails: _____

Blanket: _____

Toes: _____

Body: _____

3. Draw a picture to illustrate the sunrise.

Figurative Language

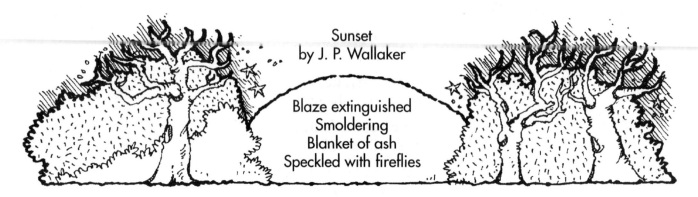

Sunset
by J. P. Wallaker

Blaze extinguished
Smoldering
Blanket of ash
Speckled with fireflies

Read the poem. Then complete the activities.

1. To what does this poem compare a sunset? _____

2. Draw a line from each line in the poem to its literal interpretation.

Blaze extinguished   the sky graying at dusk

Smoldering   the stars sparkling across the sky

Blanket of ash   the sun going below the horizon

Speckled with fireflies   the pinks, reds, purples, and oranges above the horizon

3. Draw the sequence of events described in the poem.

1	2
3	4

Figurative Language

An idiom is a figure of speech. An idiomatic phrase has a different meaning than the literal meaning of the individual words. Circle the best meaning for the underlined idiom.

1. Father asked Yana to be quiet while he was on the phone. Walter was intentionally bothering Yana. Mother told Yana to ignore Walter or she would play right into his hands.

   a. put hands on her shoulders

   b. fall into a trap that someone plans for ulterior motives

   c. make noise by playing hand instruments

2. While Zendy was reading her novel, she ran across the date when World War II began.

   a. moved quickly across a library

   b. crossed out the dates

   c. happened to find information

3. Adrian thought he was too old to help with the scavenger hunt. Melina told him to let his hair down and join in the fun.

   a. take his hair out of the rubber band

   b. relax

   c. get his hands out of his hair

4. We could hardly keep a straight face when Maddie looked at her four-year-old friend and very seriously said, "I believe you should act your age."

   a. not laugh or smile

   b. not have any curves or angles

   c. keep the drawing of a face as straight as a line

5. Brett did not tell Chelsea the secret, because he did not want her to let the cat out of the bag.

   a. tell the secret

   b. let the kitten (who was a secret) out of his backpack

   c. rip a hole in the tote bag

Answer Key

Comprehension: Fiction

Read the passage. Then, answer the questions. Use information from the text to support your answers.

In the Dark

I need to get out! It's so dark in here. It's pitch-black—no light coming through any cracks. It's like a cave. I know I'm not alone here. Weight presses in on me from all directions. I may be thin, but this is ridiculous. It's been days since any light has entered. I have to get out. There's so much noise. Everyone wants out. That whiny Blue over there . . . complaining about being down here since August. What does he expect? No one wants a broken one. Crayons aren't any fun when they're in bits and pieces. That Number Two, she gets out every once in a while. I'm not sure she's gonna make it, though. Looks awfully rough when she gets back. I swear she's getting shorter, and look at those teeth marks! Everyone else, they think they're so important. I'm the important one, though. I'm worth credit. I was supposed to be handed in over eight days ago! I can count, you know. Numbers are my specialty. Oh, I see light! There's some rustling . . . there goes Number Two again, bypassed that pack of 16. Relief. I don't feel so squashed. A hand . . . It touched me! Ooooo, numbers, feels great to be doing what I was made to do. What? That's not the answer. Phone number!?!? OUCH! YEOW! What do you think you're doing? You can't have that. You get back here right now. Nooooooooo! Darkness. I'll never get out of here.

Answer the questions and follow the directions. Highlight in the text where you found the information.
Write the number of the question where you highlight.

1. Who is speaking in this piece? **an unfinished assignment**

2. What is the setting? **inside a school desk**
   Highlight the key words or phrases in the text with yellow.

3. Who or what is Blue? **a crayon**
   Highlight the key words or phrases in the text with blue.

4. Who is Number Two? **a pencil**

5. What is wrong with her? **She is being sharpened and chewed on.**

6. What day of the week is it? (Monday)   Wednesday   Friday   Saturday

7. What happens to the speaker at the end? **Someone writes a phone number on her and tears off the piece. She is still in the desk.**

Check students' highlighting.

Comprehension: Fiction

Read the passage. Then, answer the questions. Use information from the text to support your answers.

An Ant's Life

Hal lugged the sandwich crumb through one tunnel after another. It was a relief to be out of the blazing sunlight. His downward journey was made in the company of thousands of his fellow six-footed colonists. He was tired—weary, but still going. He knew the need for food was all-important. Still, that story haunted him. The one about the grasshopper and the ant. Yes, they did have food to eat and a safe, warm home, but wasn't fun necessary, too? Hal had talked to Granny about it. "You can't fill your belly with fun or stay alive on daydreams," had been her reply. "Be happy with your existence." Hal walked slowly from the storage area, still depressed and thoughtful. A half hour wouldn't hurt, would it? He could grab extra crumbs during the rest of the day. He would still do his part. Besides, wouldn't he be more productive after having a little rest or a bit of fun? He looked towards the sunlit opening of the ant hill. A smile spread slowly across his face. There were plenty of detours available between the ant hill and that picnic.

1. What is the setting? **Inside an ant hill on a warm, sunny day.**

2. Who are the characters? **Hal, other ants, and Granny**

3. What does Hal call the other ants? **"his fellow six-footed colonists"**

4. What is Hal's problem? **Hal is tired and sick of working so hard.**

5. What is the cause of Hal's problem? **He heard the story of the grasshopper and the ant.**

6. Who did Hal talk to about his problem? How did that character respond? **Granny. She was not happy with him and told him to be satisfied with what he had.**

7. Highlight with yellow the rationale for staying and working.   **Check students' highlighting.**

8. Highlight with green the rationale for having some fun.

9. What do you think Hal will do next? Why? **Answers will vary.**

Comprehension: Fiction

Read the letter. Then, answer the questions on page 8.

Dear Jeremy,

Remember last year when we learned how good ladybugs are for plants? We found out that they eat harmful insects like aphids and the cottony-cushion scale. Some gardeners and farmers even pay to have ladybugs shipped to them for plant protection. Just a few of these beetles can eat hundreds of harmful insects from one tree, reducing the need for pesticides.

Well, my mom (who usually loves having the oval, spotted insects around our garden) has a bit of a different opinion right now. You'll never believe what happened! Our house has become one huge ladybug mansion. Mom is going bonkers!

We learned in school that ladybugs love to crawl into leaves and cracks in trees. Well, I found out that cracks in houses will do, too! When I came home last Tuesday, the sides of our house and all the screens were covered with ladybugs. They even came inside the house through cracks and around the air conditioning unit upstairs. The upstairs ceiling was covered. I found about 70 of the bugs clustered behind a curtain on a window upstairs. My sister is having a ball trying to catch them in the bathroom. She has jars filled with the little crawlies.

Mom's been calling gardening stores and searching the Internet. She found out that the beetles are attracted to light-colored buildings, especially those warmed by the sun. Boy, is she rethinking that decision to paint the house white! Once they get inside, it's hard to get rid of ladybugs. If you disturb them, they secrete a nasty-smelling yellow liquid from their leg joints. Vacuuming them up is one solution. People should also check the siding and window openings and caulk any cracks around dryer vents, windows, etc. Mom has Dad recaulking any windows that look like they have openings big (or small) enough for those little buggers.

I managed to get extra credit in science and math from this! I did some research for my science report. I learned that the two-spotted ladybug is the most common. I decided to count the spots on some of our ladybugs. Of the 256 critters I looked at, fewer than 30 had one or two spots. In fact, 197 of them had more than six spots. I looked on the Internet and found out why. Here in the northern states, ladybugs have more spots because the darker spots help them retain more heat. Pretty interesting. Sure explained what was going on at my house.

Hope you have just dust bunnies, dirt, and some candy wrappers to vacuum up at your house. If you need an extra credit project, just stop over. See you soon.

Your friend,
Ian

Comprehension: Fiction

Use the letter on page 7 to help you answer the questions.

1. What other words does Ian use in place of the word "ladybugs" in his letter? List six of them here.

beetles	**insects**	**bugs**
crawlies	**buggers**	**critters**

2. Why do you think the ladybugs chose Ian's house? Give two reasons. **They liked to crawl in the cracks. They were attracted to the light color.**
   Highlight key words and phrases in the text with green.

3. What are two ways to get rid of unwanted ladybugs?
   vacuum them up   **seal cracks with caulk**

4. How are ladybugs useful? **They eat harmful insects.**

5. When do ladybugs become a nuisance? **when they get in the house**
   Highlight key words and phrases in the text with yellow.

6. How does Ian's mother feel about ladybugs? Explain your answer. **She likes them outside in the garden. She does not like them in the house.**

7. Why did the majority of Ian's ladybugs have more than six spots? **He lives in a colder state, and the ladybugs there have more spots to help them retain heat.**

8. Where in the house did Ian and his family find ladybugs? Highlight four locations in the text with red.
   on the screens, upstairs, behind a curtain, in the bathroom

9. In this passage, Ian has chosen to research ladybugs and write a letter to his friend Jeremy. Choose a topic to research and write a letter to your teacher about your findings.
   Answers will vary.

Answer Key

Name _____ (6.RL.1, 6.RL.2, 6.RL.10)

Comprehension: Fiction

Read the interview. Then, answer the questions.

Each person in Yoriko's class was assigned to interview a professional and write a summary of the interview. Yoriko interviewed her optometrist, Dr. Iris.

Yoriko: I am interested in finding out how to care for your eyes if they have problems. What should you do if you get something in your eye? Rub it?

Dr. Iris: Never rub your eye if there is something in it. You could scratch your cornea. Pull your upper lashes gently out to lift your upper eyelid. Pull it very gently over your lower eyelashes. This can cause the object to fall out or your eyes to tear and wash out the object.

Yoriko: What if that doesn't work?

Dr. Iris: Then seek medical attention right away.

Yoriko: What if a chemical gets into your eye?

Dr. Iris: Immediately flush your eyes with warm water, preferably from a faucet, but you can also use a cup. Do this for at least 20 minutes. See a doctor or call the poison control center.

Yoriko: What should you do for a black eye?

Dr. Iris: Get a cool, wet washcloth. Press it gently on the eye for about 15 minutes every hour. It is a good idea to have a doctor check the eye for internal damage.

Yoriko: Okay, here's the gross one: what should you do if something cuts your eye or gets stuck in it?

Dr. Iris: The "getting stuck" is called penetration. If either of these things happen, DO NOT flush your eye, try to take out the object, or put any medicine on it. Gently cover the eye with gauze or a bandage and go straight to the nearest emergency room.

Yoriko: Thank you, Dr. Iris. I really learned a lot about caring for eyes.

Dr. Iris: You're welcome, Yoriko. It is important to take good care of your eyes. You only get one pair. Be sure to have your eyes checked once a year.

1. Help Yoriko with her summary. List four things Dr. Iris told her you could do when your eyes had a problem. Highlight words and phrases that support your answer.

Never rub your eye when there is something in it.

Flush your eye when you get chemicals in it.

A black eye needs a cool washcloth.

Go right to the hospital if something penetrates your eye.

2. Write a topic sentence for Yoriko's interview summary.

Answers will vary.

© Carson-Dellosa • CD-104624   9

Name _____ (6.RL.1, 6.RL.2, 6.RL.10)

Comprehension: Fiction

Have you ever heard of the "jar of life"? You only get to fill it once. Rocks are the most important things in life, like family and health. They are the things you cannot bear to live without. Pebbles are the next order of priorities: school, jobs, friends, and important items. Sand is the fun and the "stuff."

Read the poem. Then, answer the questions.

Jar of Life
by J. P. Wallaker

One jar,
Only one,
Choose.
Sand?
Lots of fun!
Room for rocks?
Pebbles first.
Rewarding . . .
What about
Fun . . . love?

First
Rocks.
Looks full.
Pebbles?
Still room.
Fill with sand.
Full . . . balance.
My jar,
One jar,
Choice.

1. What happens if you fill a jar with sand and then decide to drop in a rock? Use information from the text to support your answer.

The rock will not fit; "What about/Fun... love?"

2. What is the main idea the author is trying to tell you about the little things in life?
   ○ They aren't important; you don't need them.
   ● They are important but should not take the place of the important things in life.
   ○ They are the most important things of all.

3. In which order will you get the most of each in your jar?
   ● rocks, then pebbles, then sand
   ○ pebbles, then rocks, then sand
   ○ sand, then rocks, then pebbles

4. Which statement best summarizes what the author is trying to say?
   ○ Going to the beach is fun. Sand is the thing!
   ● Giving time to everything from those dear to you to fun is important, but it is essential to keep them in balance.
   ○ Only the "rocks" or things most important to you are essential.

10   © Carson-Dellosa • CD-104624

Name _____ (6.RL.1, 6.RL.10)

Comprehension: Fiction

Read the passage. Then, answer the questions. Use information from the text to support your answers.

Milkweed

(Maddie) stood by the side of the road. She turned over yet another pale green leaf. No caterpillar. In her other hand, covered with sticky milky fluid, was a nearly empty ice cream bucket. One lone black, yellow, and white striped caterpillar was monotonously eating larger and larger swaths out of the leaf on the milkweed stem she had placed in there for its lunch. At this rate, she would need more leaves before leaving for school in the morning. Maddie looked up. She saw her friend Jade approaching. (Jade) parked her bike. "What'cha looking for?" she asked.

"I promised my teacher I would bring in five monarch caterpillars for our first science lesson this year. I've only found one so far." Jade put down her kickstand and began to help Maddie. She looked on several milkweed leaves, then moved over to look at the stem of a dandelion.

"Don't look there," said Maddie. "Monarch caterpillars only eat milkweed leaves. I've looked over this patch twice and can't find any more."

"No problem," Jade replied. "We have a huge patch of milkweed behind our house."

1. What is the setting? **beginning of the school year, by the side of the road**

2. Who are the characters? Circle the name of each character once in the story.

3. What is the problem? **Maddie needs to find four more monarch caterpillars. She needs to find another patch of milkweed.**

4. What is your predicted solution? **They will go to Jade's backyard.**
   Highlight details in the story that helped you think of a solution. **"We have a huge patch of milkweed behind our house."**

5. Write two facts about monarch caterpillars. **Monarch caterpillars eat milkweed leaves. They have black, yellow, and white stripes.**

© Carson-Dellosa • CD-104624   11

Name _____ (6.RL.10)

Comprehension: Fiction

Read the journal entries. Then, complete the activities on page 13.

Kelli's Journal

Thursday—Shauna saw a scary movie about aliens last night. She said it was incredibly good. There were some kind of scary parts, she said, but they weren't too bad. Shauna didn't give me any details, because she didn't want to ruin the surprise for me. I just HAVE to see this movie! How can I convince my parents to let me see it? I've got to think of some good reasons for watching it.

Friday—I dropped some major hints today to my parents. I told them that there was this really great movie about aliens that we just had to see. I told them that it would be perfect for my brother Tony because he loves outer space. And after all, it's kind of educational too, right? We learn about the planets in science class. How could our parents not let us see it? Mom said that if I cleaned my room and helped around the house, we could rent the movie tomorrow night. I can hardly wait! She said that when our rooms were done, Tony and I could each invite a friend over for the movie. I promised to do what she asked. I'm so excited!

Saturday morning—Kara's coming over tonight. Mom said she'd pick up the movie and some popcorn for us. Tony invited his friend Butch to come over. I hope they stay away from us. Can't wait to watch the movie, though!

Saturday night—Ugh! I will never sleep again! Kind of scary, but not too bad—who's Shauna kidding? The movie began with rows of aliens approaching the screen, ready to invade us. In the first five minutes, 17 different alien creatures popped out and I screamed at each one! I left and went to my room. Tony and his friend will spread it all over school. I'll never live it down. Even Kara called me a chicken afterwards. I can still hear the creepy theme music in my head....

12   © Carson-Dellosa • CD-104624

© Carson-Dellosa • CD-104624   105

Answer Key

Comprehension: Fiction

Use the journal entry on page 12 to complete the activities. Write the events in the correct sequence on the event chain.

a. Kelli and Tony invite Kara and Butch.
b. Kara calls Kelli a chicken.
c. Mom agrees to the movie.
d. Kelli cleans her room.
e. Kelli talks to her mom.
f. Shauna tells Kelli about the movie.
g. They begin watching the alien movie.
h. Shauna saw the *Alien Invasion* movie.
i. Kelli goes to her room.
j. Kelli watches five minutes of the movie.

How would the final links change if an adjustment were made in link 7? Look at the change. Write three additional links to follow the new link.

Link 7: Kelli's parents decide that the kids need to choose a different movie.

Answers will vary.

Comprehension: Fiction

Read the text. Then, complete the activities on page 15.

Rolling Monsters

You are strapped in a seat. A padded bar comes down over your shoulders, allowing minimal movement. Your shoulder itches but you can't reach it. There is a sudden jerk, and you begin to move forward slowly. Your body tilts until you are looking straight up into a bank of clouds. Your body tenses. Anticipation causes your stomach to roil as you hear a steady "click, click, click" and slowly climb higher and higher. You reach the top, and the pause seems to last forever. You are catapulted forward, dropping down at a speed that forces the bile in your throat to return to your stomach. The passing wind slicks your hair back and brings tears to your eyes. The pressure stretches the skin on your face towards the back of your scalp. A lifetime of seconds and you are at the bottom, racing forward into a series of loops that won't allow your thinking brain to catch up to your emotional body. It's over. One hundred twenty seconds of adrenaline that lasted forever. You climb out of the seat on shaky legs. A relieved body and mind finally find each other. Go again? Of course. Back to the two-hour line.

Roller coasters are quick trips into total feeling and fear. Over 300 million people ride them each year to please peers or family members, to prove courage, or just for fun. Monster coasters tower over amusement parks worldwide.

Where did they come from? Russia. A country of many weather extremes found ice sledding a popular sport. In the 1400s, hills were built from wood frames and covered with hard-packed snow. Water was sprayed onto the snow to create a frozen downward pathway of increased speed. Some hills reached 70 feet high and were as steep as today's coasters. After a walk to the top, the customer rode down on a two-foot-long sled sitting on a guide's lap. Accidents did happen but the sport continued. In the 1700s, colorful lanterns allowed for night sledding in busy Saint Petersburg. People could not get enough of this sport, and wheels were added to the sleds to allow warm-weather riding.

In the 1800s, the ice slides moved to France. The warmer climate required some adjustments in thinking. Closely spaced rollers, like warehouse conveyors, were developed. The first wheeled coaster in Paris was opened in 1804. It was called the Russian Mountains. On this monster, small carriages whipped down a steep wooden hill. Many of the carriages jumped the track and caused injuries. As the years passed, more sophisticated and heart-stopping rides were developed.

Roller coasters today come in many shapes and sizes. They are found worldwide. Most people have ridden at least one and have certainly experienced the ride secondhand through television or video. Each rolling monster is out there just waiting for the chance to accelerate your heart rate.

Comprehension: Fiction

Use the passage on page 14 to complete the activities.

1. Write an alternative title for this article.

   Answers will vary.

2. What was the author's purpose in writing the first paragraph?

   to get your attention and help you experience the feeling

3. Locate four descriptive verbs used in the story. Use each verb in a sentence of your own. Underline the verb in the sentence. Be sure to use proper capitalization, punctuation, and spelling.

   Answers will vary.

4. Locate four descriptive adjectives used in the story. Use each adjective in a sentence of your own. Underline the adjective in the sentence. Be sure to use proper capitalization, punctuation, and spelling.

   Answers will vary.

Number the events below in the correct sequence from 1 to 6.

   3 Wheels were added to ice slide sleds.
   5 Russian Mountains was opened in Paris.
   6 Sophisticated rides were developed.
   1 In Russia, people made hills of wood frames covered with hard-packed snow.
   4 Ice slides moved to France.
   2 Colorful lanterns allowed night sledding in St. Petersburg.

Comprehension: Fiction

Read the passage. Then, answer the questions on page 17.

Find a Penny

Josh was walking to school with some of his friends. They saw a bright, shiny penny on the sidewalk. Josh stepped on it.

"Hey," said Anna. "Aren't you gonna pick it up?"

"Right," said Josh sarcastically. "'Find a penny pick it up, then all day you'll have good luck.' If it was a quarter, maybe . . ." He kicked it towards the sewer grate and they continued on their way.

They heard the first bell as they rounded the corner to the school. They started running. On the way up the steps, Josh wiped out and his backpack went flying. He limped down the hallway after Anna, Tio, and Zale. The last bell rang as Josh hit the door. "Tardy, Josh," said Ms. Clockswatch. "One more and you will have an extra assignment." The classroom phone rang. As Ms. Clockswatch turned her back to the doorway to answer it, Jade quietly slipped into the classroom and took her seat. She wiped her brow and gave a thumbs-up to Anna. She had narrowly escaped an extra assignment. "Let's begin by handing in our reading assignments," Ms. Clockswatch said as she turned back towards them. Josh pulled out his folder. His assignment was nowhere to be found! "But I spent three hours on it last night," he wailed.

The morning went from bad to worse. During a three-minute fact test, Josh's pencil lead fell out. Returning from the sharpener, he saw Jade put down her pencil and turn over her test. He wrote two answers and time was called. During science, his tray tipped over. Dirt, water, a plant, and science tools fell to the floor. An intercom announcement preceded the lunch bell. "The following students' artwork was selected for the City Art Fair: Haley Goodbrush, Gil Claymore, Jade Coinfinder . . ."

Jade requested a piece of pepperoni pizza. "Wow, huge slice!" she said. "Mmmm, looks good," thought Josh. He asked for one, too. "Sorry," said Mr. Vanfoods, "I just served the last one."

Josh flopped into a seat next to his friends. He eyed Jade's cheese-laden entrée. "You sure seem to be having a good day today," he muttered.

Jade laughed, "Yeah, you'll never guess what I picked up next to a sewer grate this morning . . ."

Answer Key

© Carson-Dellosa • CD-104624

Comprehension: Fiction

Use the passage on page 16 to answer the questions.

1. What kind of day is Josh having? **an unlucky day**
   Highlight specific details in the story that support your answer. **Check students' highlighting.**

2. In what paragraph do you find the event that foreshadows Josh's day?
   Paragraph 3. He kicked a penny rather than picking it up.

3. What kind of day is Jade having? **a very lucky day**
   Highlight three details in the story that support your answer.

4. What did Jade pick up? **She picked up the penny that Josh kicked away.**

5. What do you think Josh will do the next time he sees a penny? Explain your answer.
   Answers will vary.

6. This passage tells us about Josh's bad day. Write a story about a bad day you have had. Be sure to use descriptive details to describe your event.
   Answers will vary.

7. Number the events from 1 to 8 to put them in the correct sequence.
   8 Josh misses out on pepperoni pizza.
   6 Josh's science tray tips over.
   3 Jade comes into class late.
   2 Josh trips on the school steps.
   7 An announcement is made that Jade's artwork will be in the City Art Show.
   1 Josh kicks a penny.
   5 Jade completes her math facts quiz.
   4 Josh can't find his reading assignment.

Comprehension: Fiction

Read the passage. Then, answer the questions. Use information from the text to support your answers.

Theme Park

"Twenty-five, 50, 75, 80, 81, 82 . . . That's $47.82," counted Cal. He gathered the change and placed it next to the bills on the red comforter. Then he flopped back onto the bed, making the change bounce.

"Rats! We still need $13.28 to cover the admission cost," pouted Cleo. "Mom said we have to have the total cost of admission before we can go to the Greatest Theme Park Ever." The two lay on the twin beds in Cal's room, imagining the theme park: great junk food like chili dogs, cotton candy, frozen drinks, and elephant ears; grandstand games taking change and giving promises of brightly colored trinkets; and the rides, oh, the rides—wild roller coasters, water rides, and Ferris wheels.

"We won't have enough for two more weeks with our allowances," said Cal. "Besides, that doesn't leave anything for food or souvenirs."

"I know," Cleo whined, "and I've already checked between the couch cushions, under the car seats, and in all our jacket pockets." The two sat in mutual gloom. They watched the colorful leaves drop outside the window. Suddenly, an idea fell right into their greedy little heads.

1. What is the setting? **Cal's bedroom**

2. Who are the characters? Circle the name of each character once in the story.

3. What is the problem?
   They do not have enough money to go to the theme park.

4. What is your predicted solution?
   They will rake leaves to earn the money.
   Highlight details in the story that helped you think of a solution.

   Check students' highlighting.

Comprehension: Fiction

Read the passage. Then, answer the questions. Use information from the text to support your answers.

Housefly

Swak! The flyswatter hit the table for yet another near miss. A fly buzzed tauntingly just above Jeffree's head. It relaxed and landed on the edge of the window. Smik! Julia tallied her tenth kill in a row. "Absolutely no way!" yelled Jeffree. "There is no way you can get those flies every time!"

"Good thing for you I can," said Julia. "You left the sliding door open and let all those flies come right into the house. You know Mom will have a fit if they're still in here at dinnertime." Smack! Julia landed another one as if to prove her point.

Swak! Swak! Swak! Jeffree missed three more, the sweat running down his face as much from effort as from the heat. "Okay, I give. How do you do it? Last week you couldn't hit a fly if it was the size of a bird. This week you can't miss."

"It's knowledge, you know," Julia said. "I checked out a book from the library and found out something interesting about these flies—they take off backwards."

"What!?"

"Backwards. When a fly takes off, it goes backwards, then shoots off forwards. If you aim right behind their little behinds, you get them every time."

Jeffree grinned as he eyed his latest prey.

1. What is the setting? **in the kitchen on a warm day**

2. What is making the sounds "swak," "smik," and "smack"? **flyswatters**

3. What event caused flies in the house? **Jeffree left the sliding door open.**

4. Why is Julia able to hit the flies when Jeffree can't? **She is hitting the flies from behind.**

5. Who said, "What!?" How can you tell? **Jeffree said it because a new paragraph shows a different person talking.**

6. What do you predict Jeffree will do next? Highlight the relevant details in the story.
   He will aim behind the flies and have better luck.

   Check students' highlighting.

Comprehension: Fiction

Read the passage. Then, answer the questions. Use information from the text to support your answers.

Waiting

Maddie stands alone outside by the side of the road, stamping her feet. The sky begins to turn a slate gray. There are no extra colors, not even a last minute spark of light. She looks longingly at her home. The lighted windows smile warmly out at her. Maddie rubs her hands together and blows on their bluing tips. "Should have grabbed my mittens," she thinks.

Shivering neighbors slide quietly into a circle of warmth. Too sleepy to talk, they share body warmth and protection from the wind. Barren trees stand guard as they wait. A pair of wide-spaced lights approaches. The circle stirs. It is a false alarm.

A few minutes later, another pair of lights shines like eyes in the dim light. A welcoming yellow haven stops and opens, admitting the chilly youngsters into humming warmth. It moves along its ebony ribbon, between the sentinel trees to other cold huddlers and a final destination that will open the mind.

1. What time of day is it? **early morning**
   Highlight details that support your answer.

2. Why is Maddie standing by the road? **She is waiting for the school bus.**
   Highlight details that support your answer.

3. Which two words best describe Maddie? Circle them.
   (cold)   wise   (tired)   fearful

4. Who are the shivering neighbors? **other kids waiting for the bus**

5. What actually made the circle stir the first time? **another vehicle**

6. What things do the following phrases describe?
   "yellow haven" **school bus**
   "destination that will open the mind" **school**
   "ebony ribbon" **road**
   "heavy weight . . . in the middle of her back" **backpack**

Answer Key

Comprehension: Informational Text

Read the passage. Then, answer the questions. Use information from the text to support your answers.

Hammurabi's Code

One reason that modern countries run smoothly is that their laws are published. Because of this, all citizens know what laws they must follow. During ancient times, laws were not always recorded. A Babylonian king named Hammurabi created the first set of written laws for his people around 1760 BCE. He wanted to bring all of the people in his empire together under one set of laws. Because the laws were written down, everyone, whether rich or poor, was expected to obey them. Hammurabi's Code included 282 laws written in cuneiform, a type of writing in which symbols were carved into clay tablets. Each law included a penalty, or punishment, for disobeying it. The laws were written on a stela, which was a large slab of stone that was posted for all to see. Archaeologists working in the area now known as Iran discovered the stela in 1901. Spectators may view Hammurabi's Code in the Louvre Museum in Paris.

1. What is the main idea of this story?
   a. Modern countries publish their laws.
   (b.) Hammurabi's Code was an ancient set of laws.
   c. Archaeologists often find ancient materials.

2. Who was Hammurabi?
   an ancient Babylonian king who created the first set of
   written laws

3. Why did Hammurabi write down his laws?
   to bring all of the people in his empire together under one set
   of laws

4. What is a *stela*?
   a large stone posted for all to see

5. Where did archaeologists find Hammurabi's Code?
   in what is now Iran

© Carson-Dellosa • CD-104624   21

Comprehension: Informational Text

Read the passage. Then, answer the questions. Use information from the text to support your answers.

Athens and Sparta

Athens and Sparta were two important city-states in ancient Greece. A city-state is a region controlled by one city that is usually part of a larger cultural area. The citizens of both Athens and Sparta were ruled by elected assemblies. In addition, Athens had elected leaders called archons, while Sparta had kings who governed until they died or were overthrown. The people of Athens valued education and the arts and sciences. However, the people of Sparta focused on military life. Men in Sparta had to serve in the military from a young age, while men in Athens could choose whether to serve or not. The Greek city-states fought each other during the Peloponnesian War, from 431 to 404 BCE. Although Sparta defeated Athens, it was conquered later by the city of Thebes. Today, the city of Sparta is remembered for its military skill. In contrast, Athens is remembered for its philosophers and writers.

1. What is the main idea of this story?
   a. The city of Thebes was also located in Greece.
   b. Sparta's kings ruled until they died or were overthrown.
   (c.) Sparta and Athens were two very different city-states in ancient Greece.

2. What is a city-state?
   region controlled by a city that is part of a larger cultural
   area

3. How were the governments of ancient Athens and Sparta different?
   Sparta had kings, while Athens had elected leaders.

4. How were the governments of ancient Athens and Sparta similar?
   both had elected assemblies that governed the people

5. What is Athens remembered for today?
   its philosophers and writers

22   © Carson-Dellosa • CD-104624

Comprehension: Informational Text

Read the passage. Then, answer the questions. Use information from the text to support your answers.

Alexander the Great

Alexander the Great was the son of a Macedonian king. He was born in 356 BCE. Alexander learned about Greek culture from his teachers, including the famous philosopher Aristotle. Alexander became king at age 20, when his father died. He spread the Greek culture to foreign areas covering over 22 million square miles (nearly 57 million square kilometers). Alexander was an unusual ruler because he allowed people in different areas to govern themselves as long as they followed Greek customs. Alexander's empire shared a common currency and language, and many cities were named Alexandria in his honor. People from different parts of the empire, such as the Middle East and India, began to share knowledge with each other. This led to great achievements in science and art. Alexander died at age 33, and his empire was split among three generals. Alexander's empire was later absorbed into the Roman Empire.

1. What is the main idea of this story?
   (a.) Alexander the Great was an important leader in ancient times.
   b. Alexander was the son of a Macedonian king.
   c. Aristotle was a great philosopher of ancient Greece.

2. How did Alexander learn about Greek culture?
   from his teachers

3. What made Alexander an unusual leader?
   He let people govern themselves if they followed Greek customs.

4. What similarities did parts of Alexander's empire share?
   common currency and language and many cities named
   Alexandria

5. What happened to Alexander's empire after his death?
   It was divided among three generals and was later
   absorbed into the Roman Empire.

6. What does *absorbed* mean?
   incorporated, made a part of

© Carson-Dellosa • CD-104624   23

Comprehension: Informational Text

Read the passage. Then, answer the questions. Use information from the text to support your answers.

The Silk Road

The Silk Road was not really a road, nor was it made out of silk. The Silk Road is the name used to refer to the route leading from Asia to the West. People traveled along this route to trade goods, including silk and spices from China and gold and silver from Rome, Italy. Few people traveled the entire distance of the Silk Road because it was several thousand miles long and very dangerous. The route included deserts and mountains, and there was always the danger of meeting bandits. People traded with each other along the way and took goods with them to others farther along. In addition to goods, ideas and inventions were also traded along the Silk Road. Some technological innovations that travelers brought from Asia to the West included the magnetic compass and the printing press. The Italian adventurer Marco Polo was one of many travelers along the Silk Road.

1. What is the main idea of this story?
   (a.) Many goods and ideas were traded along the Silk Road.
   b. The Silk Road was long and dangerous.
   c. Marco Polo traveled along the Silk Road.

2. What was the Silk Road?
   the route from Asia to the West along which goods
   were traded

3. What did people trade along the Silk Road?
   silk, spices, gold, silver, ideas, inventions

4. Why did few people travel the entire distance of the Silk Road?
   it was too long and dangerous

5. What were two technological innovations brought from Asia to the West?
   magnetic compass, printing press

24   © Carson-Dellosa • CD-104624

Answer Key

Name _____

6.RI.1, 6.RI.2, 6.RI.4

Comprehension: Informational Text

Read the passage. Then, answer the questions. Use information from the text to support your answers.

The Tang Dynasty

For many years, China was governed by a series of dynasties, or rulers from the same family. The Tang Dynasty, which ruled from about AD 618 to 907, is considered China's Golden Age. Theater, dancing, sculpting, and painting were all very popular during this time. The capital city, Chang'an, had over one million people. Farmers were allowed to own land, although this later changed. People who wanted to work in the government had to pass a difficult exam. Only the smartest and most educated people could serve as government officials. The Tang government took a census to determine the empire's population, and households paid taxes on grain and cloth. Trade inside China and to other countries flourished because new roads and waterways made it easier to travel. Today, the Tang Dynasty is seen as a time of great cultural achievement.

1. What is the main idea of this story?
   a. The Tang government taxed grain and cloth.
   b. The Tang Dynasty lasted for nearly 300 years.
   (c.) The Tang Dynasty was a period of great cultural achievement.

2. What artistic activities were popular during the Tang Dynasty?
   theater, dancing, sculpting, painting

3. How did people become government officials?
   by passing a difficult exam

4. Why did the government take a census?
   to determine the empire's population

5. What does it mean to *flourish*?
   to grow, prosper

© Carson-Dellosa • CD-104624

25

Name _____

6.RI.1, 6.RI.2, 6.RI.4

Comprehension: Informational Text

Read the passage. Then, answer the questions. Use information from the text to support your answers.

The Trail of Tears

People of different cultures lived in North America before European explorers arrived. As Europeans began to settle the New World, they competed with Native Americans for land and other resources, such as gold. Over time, the New World was divided into states and a government was formed. The U.S. government passed laws in the 1830s making it legal to force Native Americans to relocate if settlers wanted their land. The Cherokee and other Native American groups had to move from the southeastern United States to lands farther west. Thousands of Native Americans traveled over 1,000 miles (1,600 kilometers) on foot from their homelands to the land that later became the U.S. state of Oklahoma. Many people died from disease or hunger along the route. The name "Trail of Tears" was given to this event in U.S. history because of the struggles people faced on their journeys. Today, the descendants of the survivors of the Trail of Tears make up the Cherokee Nation.

1. What is the main idea of this story?
   a. Many people from Europe settled in the New World.
   b. Some Native Americans still live in Oklahoma today.
   (c.) The Trail of Tears was a forced relocation of Native Americans in the United States.

2. What did European settlers compete with Native Americans for?
   land and resources, such as gold

3. How did the U.S. laws that were passed in the 1830s affect Native Americans?
   many had to move from their homelands

4. Where were Native Americans forced to move?
   the land that became the U.S. state of Oklahoma

5. What is the Trail of Tears?
   the relocation of Native American groups from their
   homelands to the land that became the state of Oklahoma

26   © Carson-Dellosa • CD-104624

Name _____

6.RI.1, 6.RI.2, 6.RI.4

Comprehension: Informational Text

Read the passage. Then, answer the questions. Use information from the text to support your answers.

Photosynthesis

Photosynthesis is the process in which plants use sunlight to produce food and oxygen. In addition to light, plants need water and carbohydrates to grow. A plant gathers water through its roots. It also takes in carbon dioxide from the air. A compound called chlorophyll helps plants use sunlight. Chlorophyll is what makes plants green. Plants use energy from the sun to break down the water and carbon dioxide. Through photosynthesis, plants produce oxygen and glucose. Glucose is a type of sugar that plants use for energy. Some people refer to trees as the "lungs of the planet." This is because trees help keep a balance between oxygen and carbon dioxide in the air. When people or animals breathe in oxygen, they exhale carbon dioxide. Plants convert carbon dioxide into oxygen that people and animals can breathe.

1. What is the main idea of this story?
   a. People and animals breathe in oxygen.
   b. Plants use energy from the sun.
   (c.) Photosynthesis is a process that helps plants produce food and oxygen.

2. What do plants need to grow?
   light, water, carbohydrates

3. What makes plants green?
   chlorophyll

4. What is glucose?
   a sugar that plants use for energy

5. Why are trees sometimes called the "lungs of the planet"?
   Trees convert carbon dioxide into oxygen that people and
   animals can breathe.

© Carson-Dellosa • CD-104624

27

Name _____

6.RI.1, 6.RI.4

Comprehension: Informational Text

Read the passage. Then, answer the questions. Use information from the text to support your answers.

Chambered Nautilus

The chambered nautilus is a modern living fossil. It is related to the cephalopods: octopuses, squids, and cuttlefish. Unlike its cousins, the nautilus has an external shell. The shell is made up of many chambers. The animal lives in the outermost chamber and uses the rest to regulate its buoyancy, or ability to sink and float. The chambered nautilus lives in the Indian and South Pacific Oceans. It finds its home at depths from 60 to 1,500 feet along reef walls. On dark, moonless nights, it travels closer to the surface to eat tiny fishes, shrimp, and the molted shells of spiny lobsters. The chambered nautilus cannot change color or squirt ink like its relatives, but it does have arms. Two rows of 80 to 100 small tentacles surround its head. None have suckers to hold prey, but each can touch and taste. The nautilus lives longer than other cephalopods, sometimes up to 20 years. Unlike the octopus, it mates many times during its lifetime, each time attaching eggs to rocks, coral, or the seafloor. Each egg takes a year to hatch. Humans are the main threat to this ancient creature's continued survival. Well over 5,000 living nautiluses are harvested each year to supply shell dealers.

1. Where do chambered nautiluses live? **in the Indian and South Pacific Oceans**

2. Define a *chambered nautilus*. **a modern "living fossil," related to the octopus and squid**

3. What do nautiluses eat? **tiny fish, shrimp, molted shells of spiny lobsters**

4. What happens to nautilus eggs? **They are attached to rocks, coral, or the seafloor for one year before hatching.**

5. Highlight how nautiluses are the same as other cephalopods with yellow. **They have tentacles.**
   Write one similarity here. **They live in the ocean. They lay eggs.**

6. Highlight how nautiluses are different from other cephalopods with green. **They have external shells.**
   Write one difference here. _____
   They cannot change color. They do not squirt ink.

28   © Carson-Dellosa • CD-104624

Answer Key

Name _____

Comprehension: Informational Text

Read the passage. Then, complete the activities on pages 30 and 31.

Touchpoints

Your brain is constantly making pathways and interconnecting experiences. This allows you to access vivid mental images, emotions, or even smells when you hear about, think about, or read about certain events. When you think of the word "sister" or "brother," a mental image immediately comes to mind. An emotion may also register, especially if your sister just did something nasty. Think about the word "pond." Each person gets a mental picture based on her own experience. Does yours have a white sandy beach or is grass growing down to the water's edge? Is the water clear and blue, or is the surface covered with lily pads and duckweed?

Your understanding is influenced by the previous knowledge you have tucked away into mental file cabinets. Being aware of these connecting experiences increases our understanding of new experiences. This is especially true when it comes to understanding what we read; all of our past knowledge impacts what we comprehend.

This knowledge can come from personal experience, things we have seen in electronic format, other books, or information someone else has shared with us. Each time a tie, or reference, is made between bits of mental information, it provides additional routes for retrieving it again from the billions of thoughts that have passed into our mental haystacks. Look at the example of Meg, who read two different books about boys living in the wilderness. As she was reading, Meg thought about times she had spent in woodland environments hunting with her dad, hiking with friends, or canoeing. She also thought about all of the movies, both fact and fiction, that she had seen in the past. A newscast about a missing teen also came into play, as well as numerous books Meg had read over the years. Each connection helped Meg become more involved in each book and increased her understanding and enjoyment of the two books.

1. Highlight with red four specific details about mental connections or touchpoints in the article.

2. Highlight with yellow the four places from which the past knowledge for mental connections can come.

Check students' highlighting.

Name _____

Comprehension: Informational Text

Look at the entries Meg made in her Mental Connections chart. Use the information from her chart to complete the activity below.

Event in Text	Mental Connection
Pete, the boy in the story, talks about being hungry. He finds a berry patch and picks some berries to eat. Pete talks about how tasty they are. Later, however, he gets a stomachache from eating only berries.	This reminds me of my family. Every summer we pick strawberries, raspberries, and blueberries. I know how long it can take to pick them and how delicious they are when you are hungry. Getting a stomachache is also a familiar feeling. Too many berries on an empty stomach—ouch!
Pete needs to find shelter. He looks around, but there isn't much to be found in the wilderness. He becomes panicky; he wasn't prepared to live in the wild. He finally finds a cave-like opening he can make into a place to sleep.	This reminds me of the last book I read. In that book, Neil also needs to find shelter. The difference is, he had done some research on living in the wild. I'll bet that Pete would appreciate some of Neil's books.
Pete is found. He is glad to be going home. He is also very proud that he was able to survive on his own for three months.	Learning from a difficult situation . . .

1. Look at the first entry. List two specific parallel connections.

   text: **Pete finds a berry patch and picks some berries to eat.**

   Meg: **Meg and her family pick berries every summer.**

   text: **Pete gets a stomachache from eating only berries.**

   Meg: **Meg recalls eating berries on an empty stomach and**

2. To what did Meg connect the first event? Circle your answer.   **getting a stomachache too.**

   another text   (a personal experience)

   a news incident   a TV program

3. What did Neil have that Meg believes Pete would like? **books on living in the wild**

4. Why does she think this? Use information from the text to support your answer. _____
   They would give Pete information on living in the wild.

5. Complete the last entry in the chart under "Mental Connection." _____
   Answers will vary.   **to recover or regain**

6. Based on how it is used in the last paragraph of the passage, define *retrieving*. _____

Name _____

Comprehension: Informational Text

Use this chart with the next text you read. List specific events from the text that trigger connecting memories or touchpoints. Write each event in detail in a separate box in the first column. Write the connecting memory in the second column. Be specific. Where did the memory come from?

Touchpoints

Title: _____

Author: _____

Event in Text	Mental Connection

Attribute Checklist

_____ evidence of reading book   **Answers will vary.**
_____ one event per box
_____ detailed events
_____ specific mental connections

Name _____

Comprehension: Informational Text

Read the passage. Then, answer the questions. Use information from the text to support your answers.

Migration

Some animals migrate, or move, to different areas during different seasons. They may go to warmer climates during the winter and cooler climates during the summer. Some whales swim to Hawaii in the autumn to give birth to their young in warm waters. Then, they travel to Alaska in the summer. Salmon begin their lives in freshwater streams and travel to the ocean as adults. Their bodies change so that they can survive in saltwater. When it is time to lay eggs, salmon swim back to the freshwater streams where they were born. Monarch butterflies fly thousands of miles every autumn, from the northern United States to Mexico. In the spring, they fly north again. Many birds also migrate every year. The arctic tern has the farthest journey, traveling over 22,000 miles (32,000 km) from the Arctic Circle at the North Pole to Antarctica at the South Pole.

1. What is the main idea of this story?

   (a.) Some animals migrate at different seasons of the year.

   b. The arctic tern migrates over 22,000 miles a year.

   c. Hawaii has warmer waters than Alaska.

2. List one reason why animals might migrate.

   Answers will vary.

3. Define *migrate*.

   to move to a different area

4. Where do monarch butterflies migrate every autumn?

   from the northern United States to Mexico

5. Which animal has the farthest migration each year?

   the arctic tern

Answer Key

Name

(6.RI.1, 6.RI.2, 6.RI.4)

Comprehension: Informational Text

Read the passage. Then, answer the questions. Use information from the text to support your answers.

Fireflies

Fireflies are bioluminescent insects. This means they can produce their own light. They do this by mixing chemicals in their bodies. One chemical is common to all living things; it is called ATP. The other two chemicals are luciferin and luciferase. When all three are mixed with oxygen, the firefly is able to light its lantern, or the rear part of its body. The purpose of this light is to help find a mate. Each species of firefly has a specialized code. The code is made up of the number and length of flashes, the time between flashes, and the flight pattern while flashing. After mating, the female firefly lays about 100 eggs. Several days later, the female dies. When the eggs hatch, larvae emerge. The larvae are bioluminescent and sometimes called glowworms. The larvae eat during the spring, summer, and autumn months, sleep through two winters, and then progress into the next stage of their lives. They crawl into the soil, where they metamorphose, or change, into pupas. After about two months, they emerge as adult fireflies.

Firefly light is not hot. It is, however, very bright. Catching a few fireflies and putting them in a jar (with air holes) produces enough light to read in the dark. In some countries, fireflies are caught in nets and used as lanterns. People also use fireflies in festivals and wear them in small containers as jewelry.

1. What is the topic of this article? **fireflies**

2. Define bioluminescent. **It is the ability of an organism to produce its own** How does this relate to fireflies? **light. Fireflies are bioluminescent.**

3. How do fireflies produce light? **They mix chemicals in their "lanterns."**

4. What is the purpose of this light? **It helps them find mates.**

5. The firefly life cycle has four stages. Name them. Give one detail for each stage.

   egg: female lays about 100 eggs at a time

   larva: glowworms, sleep through two winters

   pupa: in the soil adult: each species has a different light-

   flashing pattern

6. What uses have people had for fireflies? **lanterns, festivals, jewelry**

Name

(6.RI.10)

Comprehension: Informational Text

Read the passage. Then, answer the questions on page 35.

Matter Study Sheet

Matter takes up space and has mass.

Two objects cannot occupy the same space at the same time.

There are three states of matter: solid, liquid, and gas.

  solid: certain size, shape, takes up space, has mass
  liquid: certain size, shape of container, takes up space, has mass
  gas: size and shape of container, takes up space, has mass

Matter has physical properties such as flexibility, color, texture, buoyancy, smell, mass, weight, shape, and size.

Liquid + liquid: mix together, solution, or separate into levels (remember food coloring in water and column of liquids)

Solid + liquid: sink, melt, dissolve, float, or become soggy

A physical change is a change in shape, size, or state but NOT in type of matter.

  Examples of physical changes to water:

    divide water into 2 or more containers
    freeze the water (change from liquid to solid)
    melt ice (change from solid to liquid)
    boil water (change from liquid to gas)
    condensation (change from gas to liquid)
    add a substance to it, forming a mixture (remember adding pepper, rice, etc.)
    crush ice

A chemical change is a change in type of matter.

  Example: baking

Determine mass based on position of pan on a pan balance or ruler on ruler balance.

  Example: The apple has more mass because the pan is lower.

Give evidence that an item has volume. When placing an item in water, the water will rise. The difference can be measured to determine the volume.

A mixture is a combination of various types of matter in which each maintains its own properties and can be separated out (with tweezers, filter paper, sieve, etc.).

A solution is a mixture of two or more substances that cannot be separated by mechanical means (with tweezers, filter paper, sieve, etc.).

Name

(6.RI.1, 6.RI.2, 6.RI.4)

Comprehension: Informational Text

Use the information from the study sheet on page 34 to help you answer the questions.

1. What two characteristics do all states of matter share?

   There are 3 states of matter.

2. Based on the information given, which state of matter are the following materials?

   pepper **solid**   air **gas**

   apple cider **liquid**   chocolate chip **solid**

   water vapor **gas**   milk **liquid**

3. Give one more example of each state of matter.

   solid: **Answers will vary.**

   liquid:

   gas:

4. What principle of matter does this passage demonstrate? Two students, coming from opposite directions, run around a corner and crash into each other. Both end up staggering backwards.

   "Two objects cannot occupy the same space at the same time."

   Write another example of this principle.

   Examples will vary.

5. List two ways you could cause a physical change to occur to this paper.

   tear it   **fold it**

6. Are you made of matter? Give evidence to support your answer.

   Yes, I take up space and have mass.

7. You have a bowl of trail mix. It contains pretzels, raisins, peanuts, oat cereal, and chocolate chips. Is it a mixture or a solution? **a mixture**

8. Define physical change.

   A change in shape, size, or state, but NOT in type of matter.

Name

(6.RI.2)

Comprehension: Informational Text

Read the passage. Then, answer the questions. Use information from the text to support your answers.

Turn Up the Power

The ability to do work is called energy. Machines need energy or fuel to work. This energy can come from many sources. Fossil fuels like coal, gas, and oil are one important source of energy. They come from the earth and are used to fuel power plants, automobiles, and other machines. Another source of energy is wind. Wind can power windmills. It can also be converted into electricity, push gears to grind grains, or be used to pump water. Water is another key source of energy. Dams are used to harness energy from rivers and convert it into electricity. Scientists are also researching the possibility of using ocean waves and tides for energy. Finally, there is the sun, or solar energy. Solar cells can change sunlight into electricity, which can then be used to power cars, heat homes, and power electrical devices. Although fossil fuels are currently used the most, other energy sources are being used and research is being done to make them more effective and economical.

Write the topic and the main idea on the lines. Then list four major supporting details. Choose two minor supporting details for each and list them.

Topic: **Energy**

Main idea: **Energy comes from many sources.**

1. Major supporting detail: **Fossil fuels**
   A. Minor supporting detail: **Come from the earth**
   B. Minor supporting detail: **Used to fuel power plants**

2. Major supporting detail: **Wind**
   A. Minor supporting detail: **Power windmills**
   B. Minor supporting detail: **Used to pump water**

3. Major supporting detail: **Water**
   A. Minor supporting detail: **Dams convert water energy to electricity**
   B. Minor supporting detail: **Research on ocean possibilities**

4. Major supporting detail: **Sun**
   A. Minor supporting detail: **Solar cells change sunlight to electricity**
   B. Minor supporting detail: **Used to power cars**
   Answers will vary.

Answer Key

Name_____

6.RI.1, 6.RI.2

Comprehension: Informational Text

Read the passage. Then, answer the questions. Use information from the text to support your answers.

Fossils

Fossils are the remains of plants or animals from thousands of years ago that have turned to stone. After these organisms died, their bodies were buried in sediment and gradually replaced by minerals. Sometimes an animal's bones, teeth, or shell are preserved. Other times only an impression of its body is made. Footprints, eggs, and nests can also be fossilized. Fossils can be found in many places. They are often uncovered when people dig up the earth as they build roads. Many fossils are buried in layers of rock. Sometimes, fossils are exposed through erosion of a mountainside. Others are found through undersea excavation. Scientists study fossils to learn what the living animals or plants looked like. They can use radiocarbon dating to find out how old a fossil is. All living things contain carbon, so scientists measure how much carbon is left in a fossil to determine its age.

1. What is the main idea of this story?
   a. Fossils can be found in many places.
   b. Sometimes only an impression of a plant is left.
   c. Fossils are plant or animal remains from long ago.

2. What happens when something is fossilized?
   Its body is gradually replaced by minerals.

3. What parts of an animal's body might be preserved?
   bones, teeth, or shell

4. Why do scientists study fossils?
   to learn what the living animals or plants looked like

5. How does radiocarbon dating help scientists determine a fossil's age?
   Scientists measure how much carbon is left in a fossil to determine how old it is.

37

Name_____

6.RI.1, 6.RI.10

Comprehension: Informational Text

Bamboo

What do you know about bamboo? Before you read the article on pages 39 and 40, read each pair of statements. Write a **P** before the statement you predict is true based on your prior knowledge. Then read the article on the next two pages. Review your choices. Write a **V** in front of each verified answer. Write the number of the paragraph that contains the answer.

1. ____ a. There are about 100 species of bamboo.
   V b. There are over 1,000 species of bamboo.
   Answer found in paragraph **2**

2. **V** a. Bamboo is a grass.
   ____ b. Bamboo is a tree.
   Answer found in paragraph **2**

3. ____ a. Bamboo flowers once a year.
   V b. Bamboo may take 80 years to flower.
   Answer found in paragraph **3**

4. ____ a. Bamboo is grown only in China.
   V b. Bamboo is grown in both tropical and temperate climates.
   Answer found in paragraph **2**

5. ____ a. Steel has a greater tensile strength than bamboo.
   V b. Bamboo has a greater tensile strength than steel.
   Answer found in paragraph **6**

6. ____ a. One species of bamboo can grow up to 10 feet a day.
   V b. One species of bamboo can grow up to 4 feet a day.
   Answer found in paragraph **2**

7. **V** a. Bamboo can be harvested faster than rattan or softwoods.
   ____ b. Rattan can be harvested faster, but bamboo grows larger.
   Answer found in paragraph **5**

8. **V** a. Bamboo can be used to make paper, rebar, and food preservatives.
   ____ b. Bamboo can be used to make paper but not rebar or preservatives.
   Answer found in paragraph **9**

9. **V** a. Thomas Edison used bamboo in his lightbulb experiment.
   ____ b. Thomas Edison used bamboo in his telephone experiment.
   Answer found in paragraph **7**

38

Name_____

6.RI.10

Comprehension: Informational Text

Bamboo

When bamboo comes to mind, so, too, do images of pandas and China. While this plant is well known for its role in the life cycle of China's endangered pandas, it is now becoming known for its own deterioration.

Bamboo is a woody plant, but it is not a tree. It belongs to the grass family. It is the fastest growing plant on this planet. One species can grow up to four feet in 24 hours. It grows more than 30% faster than the fastest growing tree. There are over 1,000 species of bamboo. They are divided into two main types determined by their rhizome, or root, structures. Sympodial bamboos have clumps of roots and are commonly called "clumpers"; monopodial bamboos have roots that are runners and are commonly called "runners." Clumpers tend to grow in tropical climates while runners grow in temperate climates.

These fast growing plants share a unique characteristic: they rarely bloom. Each species blooms only once every 7 to 120 years, not every year like most plants. Most bamboo of the same species blooms at approximately the same time. Usually the parent plant dies soon after flowering.

Bamboo is delicate when it first emerges from the ground but soon becomes one of the most hardy plants around. The plant craves water when first planted, but within a year it can be somewhat drought tolerant. It also tolerates precipitation extremes from 30 to 250 inches of rainfall a year. One grove of bamboo even withstood the atomic blast at Hiroshima and within days sent up new shoots. It was the first regreening in that devastated area.

Bamboo has many uses. It grows fast, with some types reaching a mature height in just two months. India, China, and Burma have found that a grove of bamboo can be harvested and make a profit in as little as 3 to 5 years. This is much better than rattan, which takes 8 to 10 years to make a profit, and most softwoods, generally grown in the U.S. and Canada, which cannot be harvested for 10 to 20 years.

Bamboo is an excellent building material. It is pliable and one of the strongest building materials there is. In fact, its tensile strength is greater than steel's. Steel has a tensile strength of 23,000 psi, while bamboo's tensile strength is a superior 28,000 psi. Bamboo is also an excellent structural material for buildings in earthquake areas. In fact, after the violent 1992 earthquake in Limón, Costa Rica, only the National Bamboo Project's bamboo houses were left standing.

The history of electric lights owes much to bamboo. Thomas Edison used bamboo during his first experiment with the lightbulb. He used a piece of carbonized bamboo for the filament, or the part that glows to make light. It worked. Light was produced.

39

Name_____

6.RI.1, 6.RI.2, 6.W.4

Comprehension: Informational Text

Soil conservation is another use of bamboo. Because it becomes established quickly, it can be planted in deforested areas that have trouble with erosion. Its dense root systems hold soil in place. It can also be used to strengthen areas of land that are prone to mudslides and earthquakes.

Bamboo is used to make many items we use daily. Bamboo pulp is used to make paper. Makes you wonder if this paper originated from a tree or a grass, doesn't it? It is also used to make paneling, floor tiles, briquettes for fuel, and rebar to reinforce concrete beams. An antioxidant in pulverized bamboo bark helps prevent the growth of bacteria. This is commonly used as a natural food preservative, especially in the country of Japan.

Pandas need bamboo; it may be essential to their survival. Bamboo needs each and every one of us. When we learn to use it to its full potential, we will no longer have to watch it deteriorate or fear that it will become as endangered as the panda.

Write a summary of this article. Craft your summary statement so that each detail sentence fits the focus.

_____
_____
_____
_____
_____
_____
_____
_____
_____
_____
_____

40

Answer Key

Comprehension: Informational Text

Read the passage. Then, answer the questions. Use information from the text to support your answers.

Biomes of the World

Biomes are areas of land or water that share the same climate. Earth has several major biomes. Deserts receive little rain and have extreme temperatures. Forests receive more rain and have moderate temperatures. The trees in a deciduous forest lose their leaves every autumn. The trees in the taiga are mostly evergreens, many of which have needle-like leaves. Grasslands cover the most area of land on Earth. Rain is usually seasonal, so there is a dry season during which dust storms may be created. The tundra is located at very high elevations and near the North and South Poles. Few plants grow in the tundra, and the ground is permanently frozen. There are two types of aquatic biomes: marine and freshwater. Marine biomes cover about three-fourths of Earth's surface and include all of the world's oceans. Freshwater biomes are bodies of water such as lakes, rivers, and ponds.

1. What is the main idea of this story?
   a. Some biomes receive little rain.
   b. Deserts can be very hot or very cold.
   c. (circled) Earth has many different biomes.

2. What are biomes?
   areas of land or water that share the same climate

3. How are deserts and forests different?
   deserts have little rain and extreme temperatures, forests
   have more rain and moderate temperatures

4. What do many evergreens look like?
   Many of them have needlelike leaves.

5. What happens during the dry season in the grasslands?
   Dust storms may be created.

Comprehension: Informational Text

Read the passage. Then, answer the questions on page 43. Use information from the text to support your answers.

Go, Bones!

Most preteens do not worry about what their bodies will be like after turn 18 or 38. After all, that's OLD!! Yet there are some very simple things that can be done before age 18 that will have a huge impact on life after 50. It is as simple as exercising, eating right, and getting plenty of calcium and vitamin D, which is needed for calcium absorption.

So what's the big deal? Osteoporosis—a big word that means bones are losing mass and are more apt to break or fracture. Osteoporosis can even cause collapsed vertebrae, resulting in incredible back pain and spinal deformities like a rounded back. About half of the women and one third of the men over 50 have osteoporosis. Over 20 million Americans and over 1.4 million Canadians suffer from this condition.

Osteoporosis cannot be cured. It can be treated, but not always successfully. The best way to take care of it is to prevent it. The best time to prevent it is before the age of 18. From birth to the late teens, people build their greatest amount of bone mass. This is the time when dietary calcium—from food instead of pills—directly results in bones growing to their maximum density. If bone mass is not built during this time, it cannot be "caught up" later.

The problem is that many children are not getting enough calcium in their diets. Milk and other dairy products are rich in calcium. Several studies have shown that girls and boys who drink lots of soft drinks and fruit beverages tend to drink less milk. Other studies have shown that drinking cola and caffeinated beverages leaches calcium out of the bones, meaning that more calcium is needed to compensate. Depending on the amount of caffeine, that can mean anywhere from one to five servings of calcium being leached from the bones.

Most adults need about 1000 mg of dietary calcium per day, without drinking cola; children need slightly more. People under 18 need the equivalent of four to five glasses of milk each day. For those who don't like milk, the good news is calcium can also be found in other foods like yogurt, cheese, and some green vegetables. In fact, if you start checking labels, you will be surprised where calcium shows up.

Other preventative measures include regular exercise, a balanced diet, and no smoking. The good news is you have the power to take preventative measures now. Armed with knowledge, you can have a direct impact on what your own life will be like when you become "old."

Comprehension: Informational Text

Use the article on page 42 to answer each question. Verify your answers in the text.

1. What is osteoporosis? **loss of bone mass, which leaves bones more**
   brittle and prone to breaks

2. List two possible consequences of a person over 50 getting osteoporosis. **She may break**
   bones easily. She may form a rounded back or hump.

3. Why should kids be concerned about osteoporosis? **It can be prevented before age 18.**

4. When is the most bone mass grown? **from birth to late teens**

5. Why is milk important to this issue? **Milk has calcium, and calcium is directly**
   related to bone growth.

6. What if you do not like to drink milk? **Eat dairy products or other calcium-rich**
   foods.

7. What effect do caffeinated beverages have on the bones? **They leach calcium from the**
   bones.

8. What, besides calcium, will strengthen your bones and help prevent osteoporosis?
   exercise, eating right, and not smoking

9. Evaluate your own lifestyle. What could you do to help your bones? **Answers will vary.**

10. What is the main idea of the passage? **There are many measures you can**
    take to promote bone health. It is important to take care of
    your bones in order to prevent osteoporosis.

Comprehension: Informational Text

Penguins

What do you know about penguins? Before you read the article, read each pair of statements. Write a **P** before the statement you predict is true based on your prior knowledge. Then read the article on the next two pages. Review your choices. Write a **V** in front of each verified answer. Write the number of the paragraph(s) that contains the answer.

1. ___ a. All penguins live in Antarctica.
   _V_ b. All penguins live south of the equator.
   Answer found in paragraph **1, 6, 7**

2. _V_ a. Not all penguins are endangered.
   ___ b. All penguins are endangered.
   Answer found in paragraph **6**

3. _V_ a. Penguins have hollow bones.
   _V_ b. Penguins have dense bones.
   Answer found in paragraph **2**

4. ___ a. The king penguin is the largest species of penguins.
   _V_ b. The emperor penguin is the largest species of penguins.
   Answer found in paragraph **5**

5. _V_ a. Penguin ancestors were some of the best fliers in the world.
   ___ b. Penguin ancestors were some of the best walkers in the world.
   Answer found in paragraph **5**

6. _V_ a. Penguins can hold their breath underwater for over 15 minutes.
   ___ b. Penguins can hold their breath underwater for over 10 minutes.
   Answer found in paragraph **2**

7. ___ a. Penguins have thick, coarse, waterproof hair instead of feathers.
   _V_ b. Penguin feathers are covered with waterproofing body oil.
   Answer found in paragraph **2**

8. _V_ a. A penguin's camouflage helps it stay hidden in the ocean.
   ___ b. A penguin's camouflage helps it stay hidden in the snow.
   Answer found in paragraph **3**

9. ___ a. Male penguins are the only ones that care for the chicks.
   _V_ b. Both parents share the responsibilities of raising the chicks.
   Answer found in paragraph **4**

10. ___ a. Penguins can be found in the wild in Canada and Japan.
    _V_ b. Penguins can be found in the wild in New Zealand and South America.
    Answer found in paragraph **1, 6, 7**

Answer Key

Name_____   6.RI.10

Comprehension: Informational Text

Penguins

Penguins are interesting creatures. There are over 18 different kinds of penguins, each with its own special characteristics. However, all penguins have certain things in common. Did you know that all of these birds are located in the Southern Hemisphere? Although some live in Antarctica, not all do. Each of these birds is located in coastal areas south of the equator.

Penguins possess unique adaptations. For instance, all penguins have dense bones. Hollow bones enable most birds to fly; dense bones help penguins travel through water. Penguins also have small, tightly packed outer feathers that are covered with a special body oil to make them waterproof. Beneath the outer feathers is the down, or fluffy feathers. Under the skin is a thick layer of fat. If a penguin gets too hot, it will fluff its feathers, allowing body heat to escape. Some penguin varieties can hold their breath for nearly 20 minutes while searching for food in the southern oceans. Their mouths are filled with rough spines which help hold their diet of slippery fish, squid, and crustaceans. Their webbed feet act like small wings to assist propulsion on these excursions.

Penguins have predators which are uncommon for most birds. They include sharks, killer whales, and leopard seals. Therefore, penguins have developed a unique form of camouflage. When seen from below, their white bellies help them blend in with the sun shining on the water; when seen from above, their dark backs help them fade into the dark ocean depths.

Many penguins lay and hatch eggs in large groups called rookeries or colonies. The hen (female) lays one to two eggs, and both the hen and the cock (male) share chick-raising duties. Adult penguins have a brood patch, a featherless spot on the underside, which allows them to heat the incubating eggs or newly hatched chicks. When both parent penguins are at sea catching dinner for the little ones, the chicks may stay in a crèche, or nursery, where chicks gather for warmth and safety.

Researchers believe penguins may have been birds of flight at some time in the past. Today's penguins have evolved from seabirds called tubenoses who have nostrils located at the end of a tube on top of their beaks. Tubenoses include some of the greatest fliers in the world: albatrosses and petrels. It is believed that the earliest penguins branched from tubenoses about the time dinosaurs disappeared. The largest penguin fossil ever discovered was 5'7" tall. The *Anthropornis nordenskjoeldi* weighed nearly 300 pounds. Today's penguins are not nearly so large. The largest is the emperor penguin which stands over 3 feet tall and weighs up to 88 pounds. The second largest is the king penguin, standing about as tall as the emperor penguin but weighing only half as much.

Name_____   6.RI.1, 6.W.4, 6.L.2

Comprehension: Informational Text

All penguins in the wild today live between the equator and the South Pole. Their populations are counted in breeding pairs. Macaroni penguins account for nearly half of all penguins. They have about 11.8 million breeding pairs. Two species of Pacific Ocean penguins, the Galapagos and Humboldt penguins, are considered threatened with between 5,000 and 8,500 breeding pairs. The yellow-eyed penguin in New Zealand is an endangered species with as few as 1,600 breeding pairs.

Penguins are unusual birds. Adapted to aquatic life, their body composition and camouflage set them apart from their feathered, air-traveling cousins. Each penguin is unique, and people who cannot enjoy them in their Southern Hemispheric habitats can enjoy them in zoos or through electronic media.

Write a summary of this article. Craft your summary statement so that each detail sentence fits the focus. Be sure to use proper capitalization, punctuation, and spelling.

_____

_____

_____

_____

_____

_____

_____

_____

_____

_____

_____

Name_____   6.RI.1, 6.RI.2

Comprehension: Informational Text

Read the passage. Then, answer the questions. Use information from the text to support your answers.

Eclipses

An eclipse happens when Earth and the moon line up with the sun. A lunar eclipse occurs when Earth moves between the sun and the moon. Earth blocks some sunlight from reaching the moon, so the moon appears dark from Earth's shadow. A solar eclipse occurs when the moon moves between Earth and the sun. The moon blocks some sunlight from reaching Earth, so the sky grows dark. It is safe to view a lunar eclipse, but you should never look directly at a solar eclipse, even through sunglasses. Instead, make a pinhole projector. Cut a small square in the middle of a piece of cardboard. Place a piece of aluminum foil across it, and then poke a small hole in it so that the sun's light will shine onto another piece of cardboard. You can safely look at the sun's image on the second piece of cardboard.

1. What is the main idea of this story?
   a. You should never look directly at the sun.
   b. An eclipse happens when sunlight is blocked by Earth or the moon.
   c. The sky grows dark during a solar eclipse.

2. When does a lunar eclipse occur?
   when Earth moves between the sun and moon and blocks
   some sunlight from reaching the moon

3. What does the moon look like during a lunar eclipse?
   It is dark from Earth's shadow.

4. When does a solar eclipse occur?
   when the moon moves between Earth and the sun and
   blocks some sunlight from reaching Earth

5. How can you safely look at a solar eclipse?
   with a pinhole projector

Name_____   6.RI.1, 6.RI.2

Comprehension: Informational Text

Read the passage. Use information from the text to complete the graphic organizer.

Infectious Disease

Viral infectious disease can be as frightening today as it was in the past when it meant probable death. Viral diseases are contagious. When they are not contained, they can become a health hazard. An epidemic is an infectious disease that affects a large number of people. The infection spreads outside of a limited group and lasts for a long time. The plague or "Black Death," spread through fleas infected by black rats, is one example of an epidemic. A pandemic is even more widespread than an epidemic. A pandemic is an infectious disease that is established across the world. Smallpox is an example of a pandemic. An endemic is an infectious disease present in certain areas or populations all of the time. It is often caused by an abnormality in plant or animal life exclusive to that area. Malaria, which is transported by the mosquito, is one example of an endemic. Through time, science has developed immunizations and medications to help fight some of these diseases and treat their symptoms. But for many, there is still no cure.

Write the topic of the paragraph on the line. Write the main idea in the top oval. Write three main supporting details in the next set of ovals. Write minor details in the rectangles.

Topic: **viral infectious disease**

Viral infectious disease can become a health hazard

an epidemic affects a large number of people	a pandemic is established all over the world	an endemic is always present in certain areas or populations
lasts for a long period of time	larger than an epidemic	often caused by abnormality in plant or animal life exclusive to the area
example: plague (Black Death)	example: smallpox	example: malaria

---

Answer Key

Page 49

Name _____ 6.RI.10

Comprehension: Informational Text

Read the text. Use the map on page 50 to outline how the major and minor details work together to support the main idea.

Vertebrates

Vertebrates are animals that have backbones. Animals without backbones are called invertebrates, or "not vertebrates." There are five different kinds of vertebrates: amphibians, birds, fish, mammals, and reptiles. Each type has distinct characteristics. Some are warm-blooded, while others are cold blooded. Body coverings, habitats, reproduction, and methods of breathing differ from one to another. The one similarity that all vertebrates—no matter the shape or size—share is a skeletal structure with a backbone.

Amphibians are cold-blooded, skin-covered vertebrates. They have two distinct parts to their life cycle. The adult female lays jelly-like eggs that hatch into water creatures. Infant and juvenile amphibians have gills and spend their time in fluid environments. When they become adults, a transition is made and gills make way for lungs. Although many adult amphibians often need to stay moist, they must also breathe air. Frogs and salamanders are common examples of amphibians.

Like amphibians, birds can live around water. In fact, penguins are more comfortable in water than on land. Some of these feathered creatures, like kingfishers, even eat amphibians. Birds also live on nearly every type of land feature, and a majority spend much of their time airborne. Not all birds fly, but all birds are covered in feathers. Unlike amphibians, birds are warm-blooded. They breathe with lungs from the moment they hatch from brittle-shelled eggs. When first born, baby birds are helpless. Without parental care both while in the egg and after hatching, they would die.

Fish are lifelong water creatures. These cold-blooded animals are covered with scales and use gills to extract oxygen from the water. Most fish, like salmon, come from jelly-like eggs, but a few, such as guppies, develop inside the mother and are born alive. Fish generally do not care for their young. In fact, if a parent fish happens to come upon one of its offspring, the baby fish may become a snack.

Mammals are the only vertebrates whose females produce milk to feed their young. Nearly all mammals give birth to live young. They breathe with lungs and are warm-blooded, and most are covered with hair or fur. Because they are warm-blooded, mammals need to make their own heat, which requires additional energy and fuel in the form of food. Mammals have developed many ways to retain heat, such as thicker hair and fur in the winter months, layers of fat under the skin, and, in the case of humans, artificial coverings like clothing.

Page 50

Name _____ 6.RI.1, 6.RI.2

Comprehension: Informational Text

Although most mammals are land creatures, there is also a group of ocean-dwelling mammals. Many of these mammals are members of the whale family, such as orcas, porpoises, humpbacks, and dolphins. They live in a liquid environment and can hold their breath for long periods, but they, too, have lungs and must surface to breathe. Other types of mammals include seals, rats, kangaroos, tigers, elephants, dogs, and humans.

Reptiles are the final group of vertebrates. They are cold-blooded like amphibians and fish. They also lay eggs. Reptiles are covered with scales; some scales form shells like those of the turtle and tortoise groups. Reptiles lay leathery eggs. They also breathe with lungs. Turtles, alligators, and crocodiles spend much of their time in the water, but they are often found resting on logs or on shore, warming themselves in the midday sun.

Fill in the map. Write the main idea from the text in the top oval. Write the five major details from the text in the next set of ovals. Finally, write three minor details in the rectangles to support each of the five major details.

		vertebrates are animals with backbones		
amphibians	birds	fish	mammals	reptiles
cold-blooded	live around water or on land	cold-blooded	females produce milk	cold-blooded
skin-covered	covered with feathers	covered with scales	breathe with lungs	lay eggs
two-part life cycle	warm-blooded	breathe through gills	warm-blooded	breathe with lungs

---

Page 51

Name _____ 6.RI.1, 6.RI.2, 6.RI.10

Comprehension: Informational Text

Read the passage. Then, answer the questions. Use information from the text to support your answers.

Microscopes

A microscope is a scientific tool that helps people to see very small things. By magnifying tiny objects many times, scientists can view intricate details. Hans and Zacharias Jenssen produced a tube with magnifying lenses at either end in the late 1500s. Anton van Leeuwenhoek developed a single-lens microscope in the mid-1600s. He was the first person to describe bacteria he saw under the microscope. Early microscopes could magnify objects only up to 20 or 30 times their size, but Leeuwenhoek's device could magnify up to 200 times. Today, scientists use compound microscopes that have multiple lenses to further magnify an image up to 1,000 times. In 1931, two German scientists invented the electron microscope, which can magnify up to one million times. This device directs a beam of electrons at a cell sample to form an image that is captured on a photographic plate.

1. What is the main idea of this story?
   (a.) Scientists have developed and improved microscopes over time.
   b. Bacteria can be seen under a microscope.
   c. Compound microscopes use multiple lenses.

2. What did the device produced by Hans and Zacharias Jenssen look like?
   It was a tube with magnifying lenses at either end.

3. What was Leeuwenhoek able to describe for the first time?
   bacteria

4. How has magnification in microscopes changed over time?
   It has increased from 20 times an object's size to over one million times an object's size.

5. How does an electron microscope work?
   Electrons are directed at a cell, and the image formed is captured on a photographic plate.

Page 52

Name _____ 6.RI.1, 6.RI.10

Comprehension: Informational Text

Asthma

What do you know about asthma? Before you read the article, read each pair of statements. Write a **P** before the statement you predict is true based on your prior knowledge. Then read the article on the next two pages. Review your choices. Write a **V** in front of each verified answer. Write the number of the paragraph that contains the answer.

1. __**V**__ a. Asthma is not contagious. It is a chronic lung condition.
   _____ b. Asthma is contagious. It is caused by a virus or bacteria.
   Answer found in paragraph **2**

2. _____ a. Asthma can be cured.
   __**V**__ b. Asthma can be controlled by taking medications and avoiding triggers.
   Answer found in paragraph **3**

3. _____ a. Tight, mucus-filled bronchi won't let oxygen into the lungs.
   __**V**__ b. Tight, mucus-filled bronchi trap carbon dioxide in the lungs.
   Answer found in paragraph **5**

4. _____ a. All people with asthma have allergies.
   __**V**__ b. Some people with allergies have asthma.
   Answer found in paragraph **6**

5. __**V**__ a. Anyone can develop asthma.
   _____ b. Asthmatics are born with asthma.
   Answer found in paragraph **2**

6. _____ a. An asthmatic always has trouble breathing.
   __**V**__ b. An asthmatic can have trouble breathing when a trigger is present.
   Answer found in paragraph **5**

7. _____ a. All asthmatics have the same triggers.
   __**V**__ b. Each asthmatic has different triggers.
   Answer found in paragraph **6**

8. __**V**__ a. Asthmatics can do all the things you do as long as they monitor their breathing.
   _____ b. Asthmatics can never run, exercise, or play sports.
   Answer found in paragraph **8**

9. _____ a. Asthmatics go to the hospital each time they have trouble breathing.
   __**V**__ b. Asthmatics can usually take care of their asthma from home, working with their doctors.
   Answer found in paragraph **7**

Answer Key

Name _____

6.RI.10

Comprehension: Informational Text
Read the article. Then, answer the questions on page 54.

Asthma

1   You just found out your friend has asthma. All sorts of scary thoughts are going through your head: Can I catch it? Can my friend still do "normal" things? Is it safe to be around this person? Will my friend spend a lot of time indoors or in the hospital?

2   First of all, asthma is not contagious. You cannot catch it from someone else. It is not passed on by a bacteria or virus like the flu, strep throat, or a cold. A bacteria or virus can, however, trigger asthma symptoms in someone who already has asthma. Anyone can develop asthma, including children and adults. There is some evidence that the tendency to develop asthma may be hereditary, or passed on by parents, just like hair color or body size.

3   So, just what is asthma? Asthma is a chronic condition of one of the body's vital organs. These vital organs are the lungs. Asthma cannot be cured, but it can be managed with medications and by avoiding triggers. Asthma is an ongoing lung condition.

4   It helps to understand how the lungs work. Lungs are made up of bronchi, which are interconnecting passageways made to let oxygen and carbon dioxide pass between the body and the outside air. The bronchi branch off into smaller passageways called bronchioles. This entire system is often called the brachial tree. The bronchi are covered with cilia, which are small, hair-like projections that use mucus to sweep dust and other particles out of the lungs.

5   Asthma is a lung condition that acts differently with different people. But all asthmatics, or people with asthma, have oversensitive lungs. They have problems when the muscles surrounding the bronchi squeeze too tightly and the brachial tree produces too much mucus. This can make it hard for the asthmatic person to breathe and can also make her wheeze, or sound raspy when she breathes. Because the airways are tighter and contain extra mucus, carbon dioxide gets trapped in the lower parts of the brachial tree. It cannot get out, which results in a smaller area of the lungs being used for breathing. When oxygen is brought into the lungs, a smaller part is able to absorb it and bring it to the body. The problem is not taking in oxygen; it is the carbon dioxide trapped inside. The good news is that the lungs do not behave this way all of the time—only when a trigger is present.

6   When an asthma attack occurs, a trigger causes the airways to constrict, or get smaller, and produce more mucus, trapping carbon dioxide in the lungs. Triggers are different for each asthmatic and can include allergens, irritants, viruses or bacteria, exercise, or stress. Just because a person has an allergy does not mean he will have asthma, just as a person who has asthma does not necessarily have allergies.

7   Asthmatics can take care of their asthma at home if they work together with their doctors. An asthma attack does not have to mean a trip to the hospital. Many asthmatics have emergency medications and equipment at home: peak flow meters, inhalers, pills, and steroids. An acute attack occurs when an asthmatic cannot get his breathing under control. When this happens, a trip to the emergency room and a short stay in the hospital are necessary.

8   Asthmatics can lead "normal" lives. They can play sports, travel, and do all sorts of fun things. They do, however, need to be aware of their own triggers. Different things trigger asthma in different patients. It is not the same for everyone. Knowledge, the correct medications and equipment, and a good working relationship with a doctor are an asthmatic's best tools.

53

Name _____

6.RI.1, 6.RI.4, 6.RI.10

Comprehension: Informational Text
Answer the questions using information from the article on page 53.

1. What does the word "chronic" mean in paragraph 3? **ongoing** _____

    Highlight the answer with yellow.

2. What are bronchi? **interconnecting passageways in the lungs** _____

    Highlight the answer with green.

3. How do bronchi affect an asthmatic? **They can squeeze too tightly and trap carbon dioxide in the lungs.**

4. What is a trigger? **something that causes the airways to constrict** _____

    Highlight the answer with blue.

5. List four possible triggers.

    Answers will vary but should include four of the following: allergens, viruses, stress, irritants, bacteria, or exercise.

54

Name _____

6.RI.10

Comprehension: Informational Text
All living things proceed through a cycle of life. Each step allows the next to happen. The life cycle is continuous with enough of the species surviving each step to allow for the species to continue to live throughout time. Read the description of the plant life cycle. Use the information to complete the activities on pages 57 and 58.

Plant Life Cycle

The seed provides a safe haven for the defenseless baby plant. Each seed has three main parts: a seed coat, a cotyledon, and an embryo. The seed coat is the outer layer that surrounds the seed. It protects the seed from rough or extreme weather and from animal digestive tracts. The cotyledon, or stored food, takes up most of the space inside the seed. It will provide the germinating seed with the energy it needs to push through soil or other plant matter and provide the seedling with the nourishment it needs to begin to grow. The third part of the seed is the embryo. The embryo is the baby plant. It has an embryo root to push its way eventually out of the seed coat, an embryo stem, and embryo leaves which will later start food production.

The seed will germinate, or begin to grow, when the time is right. It requires two things to germinate: water and warmth. Water is needed to soften the seed coat so that the embryo root can poke its way out of the seed and begin its descent into the soil. New roots grow quickly, helping to absorb even more water. As the embryo plant grows, the softened seed coat splits open. Warm temperatures are needed to sustain the young plant as it grows. Temperatures that are too cold will end the life cycle by killing the plant.

Once the young plant breaks through the soil, it is called a seedling. The seedling has three main parts: roots, a stem, and seed leaves. The seed leaves are often different in shape than the rest of the leaves that will later grow on the plant. The new seedling needs three things to survive. First, it needs water in the correct amount; too much causes drowning, and too little causes it to dry up. Second, the seedling needs warm temperatures, which will allow it to grow. Third, it needs food. The seedling begins with the stored food from the seed and will eventually make its own food as it grows into a larger plant.

SEED COAT →

EMBRYO

COTYLEDON

55

Name _____

6.RI.10

Comprehension: Informational Text

As the seedling grows into a plant, many changes take place. The plant parts begin to perform their own specialized jobs. The roots grow down into the soil and hold the plant in the ground. They are the stabilizing force against wind, weather, and grazing animals. The roots also assist the plant by absorbing water and minerals from the soil. The leaves begin their kitchen job—they make and store food. Leaves use the water and minerals absorbed by the roots, carbon dioxide in the air, and sunlight to make food in their chlorophyll. This process uses the carbon dioxide produced by animals, automobiles, and factories to produce the oxygen needed by animals. The stem holds up the plant and becomes the distribution center, carrying water and minerals from the roots and produced food from the leaves to the parts of the plant that need them. These plants are found worldwide in many climates and physical conditions, from backyards to deserts to mountaintops to swamps. The list of locations is endless.

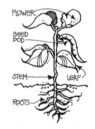
FLOWER
SEED POD
STEM
LEAF
ROOTS

Seeds are produced in specialized parts of adult plants. Seeds can be produced in cones or flowers. Cones are produced in evergreen plants. Once they have been pollinated by wind, insects, or animals, flowers develop pods, fruits, or vegetables which house the new seeds. The seeds are then scattered to a new location where the cycle can continue. They can be scattered by animals, birds, wind, water, people, or gravity. Some seeds are eaten by animals or birds and pass through their digestive tracts in their waste. Other seeds, like burs, hitch a ride in fur, feathers, or socks. People also scatter seeds intentionally in gardens. The wind blows other seeds that are specially adapted to travel like small parachutes or umbrellas. Others float on freshwater streams or ocean currents to new locations. Spherical seeds use good old gravity to drop and roll. Each method of movement ensures enough space for the new generation to grow without crowding.

Then, when the time is right, a seed will begin to germinate, a seedling will grow, and the cycle will continue.

56

Answer Key

Name _____ (6.RI.1, 6.RI.4, 6.RI.10)

Comprehension: Informational Text

Use information from the article on pages 55 and 56 to answer the questions. Verify your answers by highlighting in the text where you found the information.

Check students' highlighting.

1. Where do seed plants grow? List six places. You may use two from the article.

   Answers will vary.

2. What are some specific seed plants? List three. Example: a rose

   Answers will vary.

3. What is the purpose of the seed coat? **It protects the embryo.**

4. What needs to happen before the plant embryo can push its way out of the seed coat?

   The seed coat needs to be wet.

5. What two things could stop the life cycle of an individual plant?

   too much water, too cold

6. What are three ways that seeds can be scattered?

   wind, animals' fur, eaten and passed through waste

7. Using information from the text, define *germinate*.

   to begin to grow or develop

8. What are the roots' three main jobs?

   absorb water, make food, and hold the plant in the ground

9. Where do seeds form? **flowers and cones**

10. What are the leaves' two main jobs?

    make and store food

Name _____ (6.RI.1, 6.RI.4, 6.RI.7)

Comprehension: Informational Text

Follow the directions to create a poster of the plant life cycle. Check off each step as you complete it.

Making a Poster of the Plant Life Cycle

_____ Write "Plant Life Cycle" in the center of the paper.

_____ Write your first and last names in the bottom right corner.

_____ Divide the paper into six sections. Label them in this order: seed parts, seed germination, seedling, seed plant, seed production, and seed scattering.

(In the appropriate sections:)

_____ Draw a seed. Show and label the three parts of the seed.

_____ Draw a germinating seed.

_____ Write the two things a seed needs in order to germinate.

_____ Draw and label a seedling. Include roots, stem, and seed leaves.

_____ List the three things a seedling needs in order to grow.

_____ Draw and label a plant. Include leaves, stem, and roots.

_____ Label the two jobs of a leaf.

_____ Include the three things a leaf needs in order to make food.

_____ Label the two jobs of the root system.

_____ Label the two jobs of a stem.

_____ Draw and list the two plant parts that produce seeds.

_____ List the three things a flower can make to house its seeds.

_____ List the six ways seeds are scattered.

_____ Draw a representation of one way seeds are scattered.

_____ Draw an arrow from each section to the next.

Check students' labels and drawings.

Name _____ (6.RI.10)

Comprehension: Informational Text

Read question 1 on page 60. Then, read the passage.

Making Our World a Better Place to Call Home

"Am I in school just to learn how to be an adult?" a sixth-grader once asked. "Do I have to wait for when I'm a grown-up before I'm a person? No. I'm a person now. Maybe I can't vote for our government, but I'm still a citizen in a family and a school and a community, and in our country and our world. This is our world too, not just the adults'!"

Many children have made a difference in the world. When the American colonies fought for independence, boys and girls as young as ten years old found ways to help. Some joined the army, and others spun wool for soldiers' uniforms. Children worked together to change child labor laws so that children could go to school instead of working sixty hours a week. Children were part of the Underground Railroad that helped slaves escape to freedom. And children helped in the struggle for civil rights for all citizens of the United States.

Today, many children are doing things to improve our world. In fact, as a child, you have advantages adults don't have when it comes to making changes happen.

Children are often idealistic. They have a clear sense of right and wrong. Adults often see issues as more complicated. Children often don't have to work full-time to support themselves or their families. They have more time to devote to other projects.

Children have a lot of energy, and they can draw attention to a project. Sometimes adults don't take kids seriously when they first start trying to make important changes in their communities. However, television and newspaper reporters usually love a story about children who are working for change. And when the story gets told in the media, adults take those children seriously.

Children already have a network of possible helpers. Kids who make changes often organize their efforts in their schools. They spread the word about a project through their classes, in the lunchroom, or on the playground. Sometimes they get advisors or sponsors, and they can take advantage of the school's other resources, such as photocopy machines or meeting rooms.

All of us want to make our world better. Even kids have the power to help make that happen.

Name _____ (6.RI.1, 6.RI.2, 6.RI.3)

Comprehension: Informational Text

Use the passage on page 59 to help you answer the questions.

1. Read only the title and the first sentence of each paragraph. Which of these sentences is closest to the main idea?

   a. We should clean up our environment.

   (b) Kids don't have to wait to be adults to help make changes.

   c. Childhood is a time only for play, not for serious things.

   d. Children like drawing projects.

2. In which paragraph does the author introduce the idea of children influencing change? How does the author do this? Use information from the text to support your answer.

   Paragraph 2. He does this by discussing the idea that many children have made a difference in the world and gives specific examples, such as children working together to change child labor laws.

3. Complete each sentence with the correct word from the list.

   a. The charities worked together in a _____**network**_____.

   b. Television is one medium for news, and radio and newspapers are other _____**media**_____.

   c. He will be stronger if he will _____**devote**_____ himself to exercise.

   d. The _____**idealistic**_____ student tried to help the homeless man.

   | idealistic |
   | devote |
   | media |
   | network |

Answer Key

Comprehension: Informational Text

Read the passage. Then, answer the questions on page 62.

James Takes on Town Hall

One day, nine-year-old James Ale and his friend Bobby were playing catch in the street because they had nowhere else to play. Suddenly, a car sped around the corner and hit Bobby, breaking his leg.

James was angry that Bobby was hurt because he and his friends didn't have a safe place to play. He thought of the empty field behind the water plant. With playground equipment, a basketball court, and lights, it could be a safe park. He decided to make that park happen.

James got advice from his father and made a plan. He called the mayor and left a message. When she called back, James explained what had happened to Bobby and why the kids needed a park. The mayor said she would look into it. She called back again and explained that James's idea wouldn't work.

That's when James really went to work. He printed petitions and had kids sign them. Then he met with the mayor in person. When the mayor said there was no land available in his area, James pulled out his map on which he had marked the square of land behind the water plant. He also gave her the petition with the signatures. The mayor was impressed. A few weeks later, James met the mayor and town administrator at the site. The town administrator thought the site was too small.

James persisted. He called a reporter who wrote a story about James taking on town hall to get a park for the kids. James sent copies of the article to town officials. He kept calling the mayor to ask if there was any progress or if there was anything he could do to help.

Eventually James was invited to a town council meeting. In that meeting, the mayor announced the creation of a new park and asked James to stand and be recognized for helping to make the park happen.

Most people in Davie, Florida, now refer to that park as James Ale Park. It's the most popular playground in town. James Ale had a good idea, and he never gave up. He learned how to plan, how to organize, and how to lobby local government to make good things happen, even for kids.

Comprehension: Informational Text

Use the passage on page 61 to help you answer the questions.

1. How is the problem introduced in the passage?

The author introduces the problem in the first paragraph by

telling the reader that James' friend Bobby broke his leg.

2. Number the events in the order in which they happened.

4 The new park is used by the kids.

3 James lobbies town officials to build a park.

2 James determines that the kids need a park.

1 James's friend Bobby was hit by a car.

3. What is the main idea of the passage?

Regardless of how old you are, if you are determined and

have a plan, you can make a difference.

4. What did James do that helped him succeed?

Answers will vary.

_____

_____

_____

_____

_____

_____

Comprehension: Informational Text

Read the passage. Then, answer the questions on page 64.

Jason Builds a Library

Ten-year-old Jason Hardman loved to read, but the small rural town where he lived had no library. He decided to do something about that.

Jason went to the mayor and the town council. The mayor told him there was no money for a library, no place to put it, and no one to run it.

Jason shared his plan. The library could go in an empty room in the old rock schoolhouse. He would get people to donate books, and he would run the library. The council turned him down.

Jason didn't give up. He improved his plan and showed it to the mayor and town council again and again. Finally they agreed. He could use a room, but he wouldn't get any money or help. The room was a dingy mess, but Jason got his family and friends to help. They scrubbed the floor with wire brushes and cleaned the walls and ceiling. They added lights and built bookshelves. After hundreds of hours the room was ready.

Then Jason had to get books. He went door-to-door asking for books, and he called people in other towns. When he had 2,000 books, he opened the library.

Jason spent three hours each night running the library, but most of the time he was alone. People didn't use the library. He decided he didn't have the kinds of books people wanted to read. He wrote to publishers, politicians, and other libraries. Soon he was getting more books and more attention. A newspaper ran a story about Jason and his library. Other newspapers picked up Jason's story, and soon it was national news. Magazine writers and national talk shows interviewed the nation's youngest librarian. He testified at a congressional hearing on rural libraries. Soon publishers and people from across the country were donating books. With all the publicity and new books, more people used Jason's library. It grew so big that the town council that had rejected Jason started talking about a new building just for the library.

Within five years, the library Jason started had more than 17,000 books. Jason received awards from the governor of his state, the United States Library Commission, and even the president of the United States.

Comprehension: Informational Text

Use the passage on page 63 to help you answer the questions.

1. What is the main idea of the passage?

You can reach your goals through planning and persistence.

2. Based on this story, circle the words that describe Jason. Underline evidence in the passage.

a. lazy

(b.) persistent   **Check students' underlining.**

c. shy

(d.) visionary (seeing what is possible)

3. Think like a reporter. Fill in the blanks with the correct details from the story.

Jason _____ (who) decided his

town _____ (where) needed a

library _____ (what).

He **shared a plan with** _____ (how) the town council again and again, until they agreed.

After hundreds of hours (when) the room was ready. At first, people didn't use the library because **it did not have books they wanted to read.** (why).

He contacted publishers, politicians, and other libraries. Soon he got attention in the media, and he received thousands of books. The library became a success.

4. How is the problem introduced and developed in the passage?

The author introduces the problem in the first paragraph by

telling us that Jason loves to read, but has no library in his

town. The author elaborates and develops this problem by

describing Jason's efforts as he attempts to get a library for

his town. The author describes Jason's struggles in solving

the problem, and his perseverance.

Answer Key

Name _____

(6.RI.10)

Comprehension: Informational Text

Read question 1 on page 66. Then, read the passage.

Bullies

In the animal world, there are two reactions to bullies: fight or flight. But, you are a human being. You have more options than fight or flight. You have the ability to think and discuss your feelings with adults who can help you.

There are many ways to deal with bullies. First, think about how bullies tease or pick on people. They look for a victim and repeatedly tease the victim. Next, the victim becomes intimidated and the bully gains power. Bullies often behave this way because they are looking for a reaction. Often, bullying stems from emotions such as resentment, shame, and jealousy. Some people respond to bullies without thinking. They become angry, they obey the bully, or they become frightened. These reactions give the bully a sense of power. There are other ways to deal with bullies, such as being confident, finding support in your friends, and telling a trusted adult.

Luckily, there are many programs in place to help students deal with bullying. Over the years, many anti-bullying movements have taken place, including National Bullying Prevention Month and local movements put into place by schools and districts. Anti-bullying laws have also been put into place in many states.

As a result of bullying, some students deal with low self-esteem, depression, and feelings of loneliness. If you are being bullied or know someone that is being bullied, you should seek assistance from your teacher, school counselor, parent, or other trusted adult. You should know that you do not have to deal with bullying alone.

© Carson-Dellosa • CD-104624   65

Name _____

(6.RI.1, 6.RI.2, 6.RI.4)

Comprehension: Informational Text

Use the passage on page 65 to help you answer the questions.

1. Read only the title and the first sentence of each paragraph. Which of these sentences is closest to the main idea?
   a. Bullies are really cowards.
   b. Fighting is the only way to stop a bully.
   c. Girls are never bullies or teasers.
   (d.) There are many techniques to stop bullies from teasing.

2. An idiom is a phrase that has a meaning different than what the words say exactly. Saying that someone is "all thumbs" means someone doesn't work well with his or her hands, not that someone has extra thumbs. Which of these phrases from the story are idioms?
   a. sense of power
   b. stop and think
   c. taking a detour
   (d.) push your buttons

3. To stop being a victim, a person must break the bullying cycle. Put these phrases that describe the bullying cycle in order.

   __4__ The bully gains a sense of power.
   __1__ The bully looks for a victim.
   __3__ The victim gets angry or afraid.
   __2__ The bully teases or intimidates.

66   © Carson-Dellosa • CD-104624

Name _____

(6.RI.10)

Comprehension: Informational Text

Read the passage. Then, answer the questions on page 68.

Making Friends

Friendship is a gift you give to others, as well as to yourself. A good friend doubles your joy and halves your burdens. Good friendships make life better by what you give and what you receive.

Sometimes friendship seems to just happen. But usually, building a good friendship takes patience and continued effort. So how do you make friends?

First, make yourself available for finding and making friends. Don't get so busy with your own activities that you don't get to know other people. Homework, reading, lessons, sports, and other activities are good. But even good activities can be overdone. Spending a lot of time watching television or playing video games by yourself can keep you from developing friendships.

Next, look for possible friends whenever you are with people. Consider the other kids in your classroom or the school cafeteria. Take a class in pottery, art, karate, or whatever interests you. Join a club. Attend summer camps. Volunteer at a nursing home or animal shelter. If you are involved in things you enjoy, chances are that other people there have interests and talents in common with you. They are good candidates for friends.

Don't wait for people to talk to you. Start a simple conversation. Most people are pleased to show interest in them. If they don't respond, it's their loss. Be natural and don't worry about sounding dorky. You can discuss a class project, tell a joke, talk about a movie or the weather, ask for directions, or offer help. Once you get started, a conversation can take off on its own.

You probably know from experience that you can have many friends, but that only a few of those friends will become close friends. These friendships usually take a lot of time and effort to develop. They can start off just like other friendships, but eventually, as you talk and share experiences, some magic takes over. That's why it's important to get to know many people and put time and effort into developing friendships. You never know when one of those people will become your close and true friend.

© Carson-Dellosa • CD-104624   67

Name _____

(6.RI.1, 6.RI.2, 6.RI.4)

Comprehension: Informational Text

Use the text on page 67 to help you answer the questions.

1. What is the main idea of the story?
   a. Pottery, art, and karate classes are fun.
   (b.) Making friends takes work, but it is worth it.
   c. Talking with people is easy.
   d. Not all of your friends will be your close friends.

2. Based on the passage, which of the following statements is a fact?
   a. You can never have too many friends.
   b. A good friend doubles your joy and halves your burdens.
   (c.) You can make new friends in the classroom or in the school cafeteria.
   d. People are pleased if you show interest in them.

3. Fill in this cluster with ideas from the story.

   Answers will vary.

4. Using ideas from this story and your own ideas, make a list of things you can do to make friends.

   Answers will vary.

5. What is a *candidate*?

   a person available for a job or position

68   © Carson-Dellosa • CD-104624

© Carson-Dellosa • CD-104624

119

Answer Key

Comprehension: Informational Text

Read question 1 on page 70. Then, read the passage.

Our Favorite Animal Teammate

1. Dogs have a reputation as man's best friend, but when it comes to sports, there is no animal we play with more than horses.

2. For as long as people have used horses for work, they have also used horses for play. Some ancient games, such as polo, are still popular today. Other ancient games, such as chariot racing, have been replaced by newer horse sports.

3. The modern rodeo grew out of horse and rider skills practiced by American cowboys in the Old West. In bareback and bronc riding, riders try to stay on bucking horses. Calf roping, steer roping, team roping, and steer wrestling all require athletic, well-trained horses. In barrel racing, cowgirls race their horses at breakneck speed in a cloverleaf pattern.

4. Gymkhanas are games British cavalry riders brought from India. In vaulting, a rider swings up to mount a horse that is already moving. In flag racing, a rider on a racing horse plants a flag in a small target on the ground.

5. Fox hunting has a long history in Europe and the United States. Lately, drag hunting has become a popular replacement. Instead of chasing a fox for miles, hounds chase an artificial scent that has been dragged over the hunt area, and the riders race after the hounds.

6. Endurance events are long-distance rides ranging from 25 to 100 or more miles. Some rides include orienteering, which means using a map and compass to find your way through a wilderness.

7. Polo is probably the best known team sport for horses and riders. However, new team games have also been invented. Polocrosse is similar to lacrosse on horseback. Horseball is like basketball played on horses. A ball with several handles is used. It has to be kept off the ground at all times. Riders try to take the ball from the other team and race to their end of a field to shoot the ball into a net for a score.

8. There are dozens of other events and games where horses and riders must work together. Show jumping, steeplechasing, flat racing, harness racing, and cross-country are just a few. But probably the most popular event will always be cooperative instead of competitive—riding just for pleasure.

Comprehension: Informational Text

Use the passage on page 69 to help you answer the questions.

1. Read only the title and the first paragraph. What can you infer about the rest of the story?
   a. The story is about people and horses together in sports.
   b. **There are many different sports involving horses.** (circled)
   c. All horse sports involve racing.
   d. The story is about different animals in sports.

2. Which paragraph tells about horse sports that were adapted from other sports?
   a. paragraph 3
   b. paragraph 4
   c. paragraph 5
   d. **paragraph 7** (circled)

3. Story Puzzle

   Across
   2. open-country obstacle course
   5. extremely fast
   6. odor
   8. known for something
   10. sport of cowboys
   11. two-wheeled cart

   Down
   1. horse mounting
   3. map and compass work
   4. perseverance
   7. best-known horse sport
   9. herds cattle

   Crossword solution:
   STEEPLECHASE (across), VAULTING (down), BREAKNECK (across), ENDURANCE (down), ORIGIN/OI, SCENT (across), REPUTATION (across), POLO (down), RODEO (across), CHARIOT (across), COWBOY (down)

4. What is the main idea of this passage?

   For many years, horses have participated in sports.

Comprehension: Informational Text

Read the passage. Then, answer the questions. Use information from the text to support your answers.

Becoming a Canadian Citizen

Until 1947, people living in Canada were considered citizens of Great Britain. That year, the Canadian government passed a Citizenship Act declaring that its people were Canadian citizens. For the first time, they were able to use Canadian passports rather than British passports. Today, about 150,000 people become Canadian citizens every year. First, they must become permanent residents. This is a special legal status that says that a person has been approved to live permanently in Canada. After three years, a permanent resident is eligible to apply for Canadian citizenship. The person must be able to speak either English or French and must not have committed a crime in the past three years. The person must also pass a citizenship test to show that he or she knows Canadian history, geography, and government. After passing the test, new citizens take an oath during a citizenship ceremony declaring their allegiance to the British monarch and to Canada.

1. What is the main idea of this story?
   a. Canadians used to be British citizens.
   b. Many immigrants move to Canada each year.
   c. **People who want to become Canadian citizens must complete several steps.** (circled)

2. What did the Citizenship Act of 1947 declare?

   that people living in Canada were Canadian citizens rather than British citizens

3. Define permanent *resident*. **A person who has been given a special legal status that says they can permanently live in a country.**

4. What does it mean to become a permanent resident of Canada?

   to be approved to live permanently in Canada

5. What do citizens state when taking the oath of citizenship?

   their allegiance to the British monarch and to Canada

Comprehension: Informational Text

Read the passage. Then, answer the questions. Use information from the text to support your answers.

Languages of Canada

Canada has two official languages: English and French. Because the Constitution lists these languages as official, all federal laws must be printed in both languages. Many other languages are also spoken in Canada, including Chinese, Spanish, and Arabic. There are also over 50 Aboriginal languages, or languages spoken by natives. One or two languages are more common in different provinces or geographical regions. In some more populous provinces, such as Ontario and British Columbia, a greater variety of languages are spoken. This may be because more immigrants from other countries live in these areas and bring their native languages to Canada. Each province may choose whether to designate an official provincial language. The official language of Quebec is French. It is the primary language for over 80 percent of the people who live there. A majority of the people in the province of Nunavut speak an Inuit language.

1. What is the main idea of this story?
   a. Most people in Canada speak either English or French.
   b. Over 50 Aboriginal languages are spoken in Canada.
   c. **Canada has two official languages, but many others are also spoken in Canada.** (circled)

2. Why must all Canadian federal laws be printed in both English and French?

   because the Constitution lists these as official languages

3. What are Aboriginal languages?
   a. **languages spoken by native peoples** (circled)
   b. languages spoken only in Nunavut
   c. languages that are not written down

4. Why might more languages be spoken in some provinces than in others?

   because more immigrants live in some areas than in others

5. What is the official provincial language in Quebec?

   French

Answer Key

Worksheet 1 (page 73)

Name _____   6.RI.1, 6.RI.2, 6.RI.4

Comprehension: Informational Text

Read the passage. Then, answer the questions. Use information from the text to support your answers.

Languages of the United States

Although most people in the United States speak English, the country does not have an official language. English is used for official documents, laws, and court decisions. However, some areas require publications to be printed in another language if there are many speakers of that language living there. Thirty states have adopted English as their official language. Only one state, Hawaii, is officially bilingual. This means that the state recognizes two official languages, English and Hawaiian. Many people in the U.S. states bordering Mexico speak both English and Spanish. Other states, such as Louisiana and Maine, have a large number of French speakers. Many Native American languages are spoken on reservations, areas of land managed by native groups such as the Navajo and the Seminole. Because the United States is a nation of many immigrants, some people are reluctant to declare only one official language.

1. What is the main idea of this story?
   a. The United States has no official language, but many languages are spoken in the United States.
   b. Most people in the United States speak English.
   c. Spanish and French are spoken in some U.S. states.

2. What are some official publications for which English is used?
   documents, laws, and court decisions

3. When might a publication need to be printed in another language?
   when many people living in a location speak a language
   other than English

4. Which two states have a large number of French speakers?
   Louisiana and Maine

5. What is a reservation?
   an area of land managed by a native group, such as the
   Navajo or the Seminole

© Carson-Dellosa • CD-104624   73

Worksheet 2 (page 74)

Name _____   6.RI.1, 6.RI.2, 6.RI.9

Comprehension: Compare/Contrast

Read two campers' descriptions of waking up on Frog Pond. Then, answer the questions.

Camping on Frog Pond

Camper One We woke this morning to waves lapping the shore, a breeze rustling the leaves, and the sounds of sweet baby frogs cricking to each other. They woke the swans and ducks who sang good morning to the animals around the pond. Soon every insect, bird, and animal was calling good morning to each other. How could I stay in bed? I needed to greet the morning, too.

Camper Two We woke this morning to the incessant sound of frogs in the pond. Their shrill alarm triggered off-key honking and quacking from around the pond. The waves slapped the shore while the wind sandpapered everything in its path. Within 60 seconds, every insect, bird, and animal seemed to be protesting the hour. With this cacophony continuing, it was hardly worth going back to sleep.

1. How does Camper One feel about waking up on Frog Pond?
   She is happy and feels refreshed.
   Highlight word choices that support your answer.

2. How does Camper Two feel about waking up on Frog Pond?
   He is irritated and cranky.
   Highlight word choices that support your answer.

3. After reading both pieces, state four facts about what happened at Frog Pond that morning. Do not include any opinion words.
   Frogs were croaking in the morning. Swans and ducks made
   sounds too. The wind was blowing and it created waves.
   Insects and other animals began to make sounds too.

4. What is the main idea of each passage?
   Camper One: Waking up on the pond can be refreshing.
   Camper Two: Waking up on the pond can be irritating.

5. How does each author present his or her view of the pond?
   Answers will vary.

74   © Carson-Dellosa • CD-104624

Worksheet 3 (page 75)

Name _____   6.RI.10

Comprehension: Compare/Contrast

Read the two passages on pages 75 and 76 about making change happen. As you read, think about how the two authors present the topic of change.

Organizing to Make Change Happen

What do you see that needs changing? Is it something in your neighborhood? Or is it something much bigger? Whatever it is, by using some imagination and having faith in yourself, you can make a difference. Perhaps your efforts will help only one person. That's great. But maybe your efforts will benefit a whole community of living things: plants, animals, or human beings.

One person can make a difference. However, usually a group of people can make a bigger difference. If you feel strongly about an issue, there are probably other kids who feel the same way. Organize a group to work on the problem.

Group work will be more effective if you do four things: (1) Write a mission statement that defines exactly what you want to accomplish. (2) Schedule regular meetings. (3) Give each person a responsibility. (4) Make the work fun!

Adult advisors can help. They have more access to resources. Make certain to choose adults who will help but who will not try to take over.

Knowledge is power. The more you know about your cause, the better. Make a long list of questions. What is the real problem? Who is responsible? What laws apply? How much money would it take to make a change?

Then research answers to your questions. The Internet can be a good place to start, but don't overlook your public library. Many libraries have staff that can help you find answers. Also, develop your own information. Gather statistics by observation and interviews. Try to understand all sides of the issue.

Once you understand all sides of the issue, you still feel strongly about the need for change, develop a plan of action. Your goal is the heart of your plan. Break down your goal into smaller objectives. Then make assignments. Each objective should have a person who is responsible for it and a deadline. Finally, do the work you need to do to make sure your plan stays on schedule.

With passion for change, knowledge, the help of others, and a plan, you are on your way to making a difference in the world.

© Carson-Dellosa • CD-104624   75

Worksheet 4 (page 76)

Name _____   6.RI.10

Comprehension: Compare/Contrast

Tools for Making Change Happen

If you want to bring about positive change in your world, you need to take action. Here are some of the tools you can use.

Use Petitions. A petition states the problem and the changes you propose. It includes signatures of people who agree with you. Petitions show decision makers and the media how many people want the change.

Use the Media. Newspaper and television reporters need interesting stories for their readers and viewers. Contact reporters who cover your issue and show them why your story is interesting.

Build a Website. Organize your research on the problem. Create a website about the problem and the changes that should be made. Use keywords about the issue in your titles so search engines can find you.

Send Letters, Postcards, and Emails. Use letters, postcards, and emails to explain the problem, propose changes, ask for support, or thank people. Target people who should be interested. Be respectful.

Speak to Groups. If you are concerned about a local issue, the town meeting is a good place to be heard. Your comments will become part of the public record. Clubs and other organizations also look for good speakers.

Work with Elected Officials. Officials are elected to make things better for their community. Find an official who is interested in your issue. Then work together to solve the problem.

Negotiate. If you are trying to get an organization to change, you may need to negotiate. Know exactly what you want changed, but also know what smaller changes would be good for now.

Boycott. To boycott is to not buy products from a company you think is doing something wrong. Make sure your facts are correct. Then get as many people as possible to join the boycott. It can be a powerful tool for change.

Demonstrate and Protest. If your other tools aren't working, or if the problem is urgent, you may consider demonstrating: marching, picketing, and carrying signs. Be creative if you want to draw attention to the issue and help educate and influence people. Also, be aware of any laws about demonstrations or meetings that you will need to obey. Make sure what you are doing does not cause harm.

Sometimes kids see problems adults overlook. Kids can gain real power to make good changes when they organize and use the right tools to get their message out.

76   © Carson-Dellosa • CD-104624

© Carson-Dellosa • CD-104624   121

Answer Key

Name _____   (6.RI.1, 6.RI.2, 6.RI.9)

Comprehension: Compare/Contrast

Use the passage on page 75 to answer the questions.

1. Based on this story, which of these statements are true?
   a. Only a group of people can make change happen.
   (b.) A person has to understand all sides of an issue before acting.
   (c.) Our world improves as people work to improve it.
   d. Only adults should be the leaders of groups working for change.

2. Based on paragraph seven, which of these statements are true?
   (a.) A goal is the one main objective.
   (b.) A goal can be broken down into smaller parts or objectives.
   c. A good leader does all of the work alone.
   (d.) A plan of action should include deadlines and a schedule.

3. What is an *objective*?
   a goal or target

4. Make a list of things you see that should be improved in your area or in our world.
   Answers will vary.

5. What is the main idea of this passage?
   You can be effective at making a change if you are organized and have a plan.

Name _____   (6.RI.1, 6.RI.2, 6.RI.9)

Comprehension: Compare/Contrast

Use the passage on page 76 to answer the questions.

1. Based on this story, which of these statements are true?
   (a.) Letters and emails can be used to gather financial support for a cause.
   b. Being obnoxious is the best way to get support for a cause.
   (c.) Kids can help improve our world.
   d. Kids can never be speakers in town meetings.

2. Match the cause on the left with its main effect on the right.
   4 A large group boycotts a product.
   3 A person has petitions signed.
   2 A small group demonstrates in a busy public area.
   1 A person works with an elected official on a legal issue.

   > 1. A bill is introduced to change a law.
   > 2. People become aware of the issue.
   > 3. Decision makers know that many people are interested in the issue.
   > 4. The company loses sales.

3. What is the main idea of this passage?
   There are many tools you can use to bring about positive change.

4. Reread the passages on pages 75 and 76. Compare and contrast how each author presents the topic of change. How are the passages similar? How are they different?
   Answers will vary.

Name _____   (6.RI.1, 6.RI.2, 6.RI.10)

Comprehension: Compare/Contrast

Read the passages on pages 79 and 80. Then, answer the questions. Use information from the text to support your answers.

Exploring Space

People have been fascinated by outer space for centuries. The first animals sent into space were fruit flies, which traveled on a U.S. rocket in 1947. Many countries sent monkeys into space to investigate how space travel might affect humans. A Russian dog named Laika became the first animal to orbit Earth in 1957. In 1961, the Russian cosmonaut Yuri Gagarin became the first person to travel into space. His spacecraft orbited Earth once and then landed. In 1969, the American astronaut Neil Armstrong became the first person to walk on the moon. The United States developed a space shuttle during the 1980s that could be used many times, like an airplane. Russia built a space station called Mir that was used for many years. Astronauts began assembling the International Space Station in 1998. This research station is a cooperative project among many countries, including the United States, Russia, Japan, Brazil, Canada, and 11 European countries.

1. What is the main idea of this story?
   a. People have always been fascinated by outer space.
   (b.) Space travel has improved greatly over the past several decades.
   c. Mir was a Russian space station.

2. Why did many countries send monkeys into space?
   to see how space travel might affect humans

3. Who was the first person to travel into space?
   Yuri Gagarin

4. What was significant about the space shuttle?
   It could be used many times and is like an airplane.

5. What is the International Space Station?
   a research station that many countries are working together to build

---

Name _____   (6.RI.1, 6.RI.9, 6.RI.10)

Comprehension: Compare/Contrast

Read the text. Then, answer the questions.

Moon Beverage

Space travel has long captured the human imagination. Rocket into space and explore the star-infested darkness! Drop down on Mars, perhaps Jupiter and Saturn! Ready to take off? Sorry, it is currently impossible. Problems include finding ways to transport oxygen for breathing and fuel for traveling. But the Moon and a frozen earth beverage may soon help solve some of these problems.

In 1998, NASA launched the Lunar Prospector on a 19-month mission. This spacecraft's job was to map and explore the Moon from orbit, then make a controlled landing on the Moon's south pole. It had many specialized instruments onboard to assist with its mission. One instrument, called the neutron spectrometer, was designed to detect minute amounts of water ice. In 1998, the Lunar Prospector collected information indicating the likelihood of solid water existing on the Moon.

The mission determined that frozen pockets of water are most likely located in many of the Moon's craters. These deep craters have areas that are in bitterly frigid constant darkness. These craters, well below 0°F, are definitely cold enough to freeze and keep frozen water, which freezes at just 32°F.

What makes water such a precious beverage? It is made up of two hydrogen molecules and one oxygen molecule. The water on the Moon could be separated and used to provide oxygen for breathing and hydrogen for fuel. Where could this water have come from? No one is certain, but many scientists believe it came from space debris that has bombarded the Moon over time. Is a manned station planned for any time soon? Information will need to be studied, hypotheses confirmed, then . . . possibly.

1. What problems currently stop space travel? **means of transporting oxygen and fuel**

2. Highlight three facts about the Lunar Prospector stated in the text. **Answers will vary.**

3. What is a neutron spectrometer? **an instrument designed to detect ice**

4. What were the Lunar Prospector's findings regarding frozen water? **it is very probable it is there**

5. Why is finding water important? **It can be used to make oxygen and fuel.**

6. If there is water on the Moon, how did it get there? **space debris hitting the moon**

7. On another sheet of paper, compare and contrast how each author presents the topic of space travel. How are the passages similar? How are they different?
   Answers will vary.

© Carson-Dellosa • CD-104624

Answer Key

Name _____ (6.RI.1, 6.RI.7, 6.RI.10)

Comprehension: Integrating Knowledge
Bicycle Safety

Faiza presented a report on bicycle safety to her class. She polled her classmates about their own bicycle safety before and after her presentation. She then compiled the two frequency tables below. In her report, Faiza included safety rules and read statistics on bicycle-related injuries and deaths each year. She also pointed out that one of the most critical safety issues was wearing a helmet every time you ride a bicycle.

Safety before Report	Yes	No
Do you think you will always check your brakes, seat, handlebars, and tires before riding?	1	24
Do you think you will always wear a helmet?	9	16
Do you think you will always pay attention to all traffic signs?	12	13
Do you think you will regularly ride on the handlebars or with two people on a bike?	10	15
Do you think you will always walk your bike across busy intersections?	3	22

Prediction after Report	Yes	No
Do you think you will always check your brakes, seat, handlebars, and tires before riding?	16	9
Do you think you will always wear a helmet?	22	3
Do you think you will always pay attention to all traffic signs?	22	3
Do you think you will regularly ride on the handlebars or with two people on a bike?	2	23
Do you think you will always walk your bike across busy intersections?	22	3

Use the information above to answer the following questions.

1. Compare both sets of data. Write two true, specific statements comparing them. Use information from the text to support your answer. **Answers will vary. Example: More students thought they would wear a helmet after the report than before it.**

2. Based on the data, what conclusion could Faiza make about her report?
   - (a.) Her report influenced her classmates.
   - b. Her report was about safety.
   - c. Her report did not get a passing grade.

3. Which details in Faiza's report may have caused the post-report results?
   statistics about bicycle-related injuries and deaths

81

Name _____ (6.RI.10)

Comprehension: Integrating Knowledge
Read the passage. Then, answer the questions on page 83.

Great Lakes

The Great Lakes, located in North America, are the largest bodies of fresh water in the world. It is generally believed that they were made by glaciers that once covered the area. As the glaciers retreated, they gouged and filled the five Great Lakes as well as many other smaller lakes and rivers in the area.

Today, the Great Lakes are shared by two countries: the United States and Canada. The lakes provide people in the area with fresh water for drinking and for use in the home. They also assist many power plants and manufacturing companies. Recreation and transportation are two additional benefits. These lakes are also home to numerous freshwater fish like salmon, perch, trout, and walleye.

Lake Superior is the deepest of the five lakes. It also lies the farthest north. This lake is cold year-round and can develop violent storms. Because of this, many ships lie at the bottom of Lake Superior, including the famous *Edmund Fitzgerald*. The Soo Locks, completed in 1855, connect Lake Superior to Lake Huron, which is over 20 feet lower. The locks were built to transport large ships and goods. Lake Superior is the largest freshwater lake in the world.

Lake Huron is named for an Indian tribe that once lived along its shores. This lake has more islands than any of the other four Great Lakes. Most of these islands are nearer to the Canadian border than the Michigan border. Lake Huron touches Lake Superior at the Soo Locks, Lake Michigan at the Straits of Mackinac, and Lake Erie to the south.

Lake Michigan is the only Great Lake located entirely within the United States. The rest share boundaries with Canada and the U.S. Lake Michigan borders Wisconsin, Illinois, Indiana, and Michigan.

Lake Erie reaches the farthest south of any of the Great Lakes. It is also the shallowest. The most eastern Great Lake is Lake Ontario.

Name _____ (6.RI.1, 6.RI.7, 6.RI.10)

Comprehension: Integrating Knowledge
Use the passage on page 82 to answer the questions.

1. How were the Great Lakes formed?
   Glaciers once covered the area. As the glaciers retreated, they gouged out the land and filled them as the ice melted.

2. How are the Great Lakes used by the people living on their borders?
   People use the water in their homes and for drinking. The water also provides power, recreation, and a means for transportation.

Use the clues below and information in the text and map to assist you in completing the problem-solving matrix below.

- The deepest Great Lake is also the largest.
- A lake that connects at the Straits of Mackinac has the second largest area.
- The shallowest lake is not the smallest in area.
- The lake without a Canadian border has the third largest area.

		Area (in square miles)				
		7,320	9,910	22,300	23,000	31,700
Great Lakes	Erie		✔			
	Huron				✔	
	Michigan			✔		
	Ontario	✔				
	Superior					✔

Lake Erie covers **9,910** square miles.

Lake Huron covers **23,000** square miles.

Lake Michigan covers **22,300** square miles.

Lake Ontario covers **7,320** square miles.

Lake Superior covers **31,700** square miles.

83

Name _____ (6.RI.1, 6.RI.4, 6.RI.7)

Comprehension: Integrating Knowledge
Read the passage and the table. Then, answer the questions on pages 84 and 85.

Sleep Tight

Getting enough sleep is extremely important. This is the time the heart, lungs, muscles, nervous system, digestive system, and skeletal system get a chance to rest and get ready for another busy day. Insufficient sleep results in a sleep debt, or an amount of sleep owed your body. Sleep debt definitely affects the way a person functions. People with this deficit may not think they are sleepy, but they are less able to concentrate. They are also irritable and emotional and may have trouble reacting. In fact, some people with a sleep debt can act in ways that mimic the symptoms of attention deficit disorder (ADD). Uninterrupted sleep in which the sleeper reaches and maintains REM, or rapid eye movement, sleep is the key. It is in this stage of sleep that the body and brain get the relief needed in order to function at their optimum levels the next day. Every individual has his own sleep needs, but researchers have determined the approximate amount of sleep needed by school-age children. These times do not include time spent reading in bed, talking, or thinking about the next day. Add to the times below the amount of time it takes you to fall asleep.

Amount of sleep needed by school-age children	
Age	Suggested hours of uninterrupted sleep
1–6 years old	10–12 hours
6–12 years old	9–11 hours
12–18 years old	8–10 hours

1. According to this table, if an 11-year-old gets up at 6:30 a.m., what is the latest time she should fall asleep?
   9:30 P.M.

2. What is a "sleep debt"? **an amount of sleep owed your body**

3. Why is sleep so important?
   It gives your body a chance to rest and get ready for a new day.

4. What happens to a person who does not get enough sleep? Name two effects.
   He may become irritable and emotional. He may not be able to concentrate.

5. What type of sleep is the most important for your body? **uninterrupted REM sleep**

Answer Key

Name _____   6.RI.1, 6.RI.4, 6.RI.7

Comprehension: Integrating Knowledge

6. According to the table, how much sleep should you get each night?

9–11 or 8–10, depending on age

7. What time do you get up in the morning? **Answers will vary.**

What is the latest you should fall asleep each night? _____

8. If you were to get the greatest amount of recommended sleep,

what time would you fall asleep? **Answers will vary.**

9. What time did you go to sleep last night? **Answers will vary.**

According to the table, did you get enough sleep? _____

Use the graph to record the amount of sleep you get over the course of one week. List the days across the bottom. Begin with the number of hours you slept last night. **Graphs will vary.**

Hours

Days of the Week

Evaluate your graph. Write two true statements based upon the data you collected.

_____

© Carson-Dellosa • CD-104624   85

Name _____   6.L.4a, 6.L.6

Context Clues

Read the sentences below. Choose the word in the word box that is a synonym, or word with nearly the same meaning, for the boldfaced word. Then, write it on the line below the sentence.

considered	told	increase	threatened	critical
document	billfold	collecting	empty	

1. The storyteller **narrated** the tale in a deep, booming voice.
   told

2. I received a **certificate** that said I had successfully completed the course.
   document

3. The mayor said that providing funding for the hospital was an **urgent** issue.
   critical

4. The judge **contemplated** the evidence before making her decision.
   considered

5. That house has been **vacant** for several months.
   empty

6. Dad took a $10 bill out of his **wallet** and handed it to the clerk.
   billfold

7. The habitat of many animals is **endangered**.
   threatened

8. My uncle has been **accumulating** baseball cards since he was a child.
   collecting

9. The large speakers **amplify** the volume of the music.
   increase

86   © Carson-Dellosa • CD-104624

Name _____   6.L.4a, 6.L.6

Context Clues

Read the sentences below. Choose the word in the word box that is a synonym for the boldfaced word. Then, write it on the line below the sentence.

bendable	achieve	quick	greatest	bright
cautiously	feed	hobby	forceful	

1. Grandpa likes to wear shirts with **vivid** colors when he plays golf.
   bright

2. The children's toy is made out of **flexible** plastic.
   bendable

3. My favorite **pastime** is painting pictures of flowers using watercolors.
   hobby

4. Mom **gingerly** opened the door to find out where the noise was coming from.
   cautiously

5. If you work hard, you can **attain** any goal.
   achieve

6. The announcer told us in an **emphatic** voice that the train was about to depart.
   forceful

7. The **maximum** number of students in a class at my sister's school is 22.
   greatest

8. It is important to **nourish** your body with healthy foods.
   feed

9. Cherie walked across the room with a **brisk** stride.
   quick

© Carson-Dellosa • CD-104624   87

Name _____   6.L.4a, 6.L.6

Context Clues

Read the sentences below. Choose the word in the word box that is a synonym, or word with nearly the same meaning, for the boldfaced word. Then, write it on the line below the sentence.

peaceful	spines	nimble	slight	eagerness
beautiful	certain	confused	exact	

1. The weather forecaster said that there was only a **scant** chance of rain.
   slight

2. I was **perplexed** by the math problem at first, but then it began to make sense.
   confused

3. The pond was very **tranquil** at sunset.
   peaceful

4. Rita's gold necklace is **exquisite**.
   beautiful

5. We were asked to give a **literal** translation of the Spanish phrase.
   exact

6. A hedgehog's **bristles** help protect it from predators.
   spines

7. Our coach felt **confident** that we could win the game.
   certain

8. The gymnast was very **agile** on the balance beam.
   nimble

9. Abel has a great **fervor** for learning and spends every Saturday at the library.
   eagerness

88   © Carson-Dellosa • CD-104624

© Carson-Dellosa • CD-104624

Answer Key

Name _____ ⟨6.L.4a, 6.L.6⟩

Context Clues

Read the sentences below. Use the context clues to figure out the definition of each boldfaced word. Then write the letter of the correct definition on the line.

a. showed how	f. able to be changed
b. people who move from another country	g. provide nutrients
c. decision	h. usually
d. made shorter	i. mechanical device
e. plans	j. forecasted

1. The word *doctor* can be **abbreviated** as *Dr.* __D__

2. Ms. Yang **demonstrated** how to complete the experiment. __A__

3. My brother and I **typically** spend each summer at our grandmother's house. __H__

4. The sportscaster **predicted** that the visiting team would win the game. __J__

5. My **schedule** includes activities every day after school. __E__

6. The coach asked us to keep our plans **flexible** in case our team made the playoffs. __F__

7. Eating a variety of foods helps to **nourish** the body. __G__

8. My mother's parents were **immigrants** from Russia. __B__

9. Mom fixed the **mechanism** so that she could move the garage door up and down. __I__

10. The judge said that she had reached a **verdict**. __C__

© Carson-Dellosa • CD-104624   89

Name _____ ⟨6.L.4a, 6.L.6⟩

Context Clues

Read the sentences below. Use the context clues to figure out the definition of each boldfaced word. Then, write the letter of the correct definition on the line.

a. a part played by an actor	f. satisfied
b. at the edge	g. at the same time
c. common saying	h. pull out
d. left out	i. took back
e. characteristics of a surface	j. stages

1. My uncle used a hammer to **wrench** the nail out of the board. __H__

2. Daniel tried out for a **role** in the school play. __A__

3. Silk has a very smooth **texture**. __E__

4. Our class called out the answer to the question in **unison**. __G__

5. I **retrieved** my hat from the lost-and-found box. __I__

6. We learned about the **phases** of the moon in science class. __J__

7. Tony **quenched** his thirst after the race by drinking water. __F__

8. The scientists believed that they were on the **verge** of finding a cure for the disease. __B__

9. An old **maxim** is "A stitch in time saves nine." __C__

10. The teacher accidentally **omitted** Cathy's name from the list. __D__

90   © Carson-Dellosa • CD-104624

Name _____ ⟨6.L.4a, 6.L.6⟩

Context Clues

Read the sentences below. Use the context clues to figure out the definition of each boldfaced word. Then, write the letter of the correct definition on the line.

a. put forward	f. pushed by bumping
b. not well-known	g. in part
c. manner of walking	h. to begin or start
d. wool	i. noticed
e. book about a person's life	j. figured out

1. Our assignment is to write a summary of a **biography**. __E__

2. Mia **asserted** her opinion at the meeting. __A__

3. Please take your seats because the presentation is about to **commence**. __H__

4. We **deduced** the answer to the problem. __J__

5. The topic of her report is an **obscure** painter from the Middle Ages. __B__

6. My project is only **partially** complete. __G__

7. Amanda has a very fast **gait**, so it is hard to keep up with her. __C__

8. My arm was **jostled** when someone tried to move past me in the crowd. __F__

9. The science teacher asked us to write everything we **perceived**. __I__

10. The sheep's **fleece** was thick. __D__

© Carson-Dellosa • CD-104624   91

Name _____ ⟨6.L.4b, 6.L.6⟩

Greek and Latin Roots

Many English words contain roots from other languages such as Greek and Latin. For example, the word *monarch* contains the roots *mon*, meaning "one," and *arch*, meaning "ruler." Therefore, a *monarch* is "one ruler," or a person who rules a country alone. Read the list of roots below.

bio: life	**ast:** star	**zoo:** animals	**geo:** earth
psych: mind	**archaeo:** ancient	**bot:** plant	**anthrop:** human

Use these roots to help you match the following words with their meanings.

archaeologist	zoologist	psychologist	biologist
anthropologist	botanist	astronomer	geologist

1. scientist who studies plants _____ **botanist**

2. scientist who studies the human mind _____ **psychologist**

3. scientist who studies ancient people _____ **archaeologist**

4. scientist who studies different life forms _____ **biologist**

5. scientist who studies the earth _____ **geologist**

6. scientist who studies human cultures _____ **anthropologist**

7. scientist who studies the solar system _____ **astronomer**

8. scientist who studies animals _____ **zoologist**

92   © Carson-Dellosa • CD-104624

Answer Key

Worksheet 1 (page 93)

Name _____ 6.L.4b, 6.L.6

Greek and Latin Roots

Many English words contain roots from other languages such as Greek and Latin. For example, the word *thermometer* contains the roots *therm* and *meter. Therm* means "heat," and *meter* means "to measure." Therefore, a *thermometer* is a device that measures heat. Read the list of roots below.

dent: tooth	**cardi:** heart	**neur:** nerve	**pod:** foot
hemo: blood	**ped:** child	**opt:** eye	**derm:** skin

Use these roots to match the following words with their meanings. Write the correct word in each blank.

cardiologist	hematologist	dermatologist	pediatrician
ophthalmologist	neurologist	podiatrist	dentist

1. doctor who examines blood **hematologist**
2. doctor who examines feet **podiatrist**
3. doctor who examines children **pediatrician**
4. doctor who examines teeth **dentist**
5. doctor who examines the nervous system **neurologist**
6. doctor who examines skin **dermatologist**
7. doctor who examines the heart **cardiologist**
8. doctor who examines eyes **ophthalmologist**

© Carson-Dellosa • CD-104624   93

Worksheet 2 (page 94)

Name _____ 6.L.4b, 6.L.6

Greek and Latin Roots

Many English words contain roots from other languages such as Greek and Latin. For example, the word *bicycle* contains the roots *bi* and *cycl. Bi* means "two," and *cycl* means "a circle or ring." Therefore, a *bicycle* is a vehicle that has two circles, or wheels. Read the list of roots below.

omni: all	**nutri:** nourish	**herba:** grass	**spir:** breathe
phys: body, nature	**carn:** meat	**aero:** air	**chlor:** green

Use these roots to help you match the following words with their meanings.

herbivore	nutrition	physical	respiration
aerobic	carnivore	chlorophyll	omnivore

1. something that makes plants' leaves green **chlorophyll**
2. animal that eats only plants **herbivore**
3. taking in the food necessary for health and growth **nutrition**
4. the act of breathing **respiration**
5. animal that eats only meat **carnivore**
6. helping the body take in more oxygen **aerobic**
7. relating to the body **physical**
8. animal that eats all kinds of food **omnivore**

94   © Carson-Dellosa • CD-104624

Worksheet 3 (page 95)

Name _____ 6.L.4b, 6.L.6

Greek and Latin Roots

Many English words contain roots from other languages such as Greek and Latin. For example, the word *submarine* contains the roots *sub* and *marine. Sub* means "below," and *marine* means "water." Therefore, a *submarine* is a vehicle that travels below the water. Read the list of roots below.

ann: year	**auto:** self	**loc:** place	**chron:** time
dem: people	**fac:** make	**spec:** see	**biblio:** book

Use these roots to match the following words with their meanings.

democracy	bibliography	location	chronology
factory	spectator	anniversary	autobiography

1. place where things are made **factory**
2. position of something **location**
3. date marking a yearly event **anniversary**
4. person who watches something **spectator**
5. list of events in order **chronology**
6. book about a person's own life **autobiography**
7. government by the people **democracy**
8. list of reference books **bibliography**

© Carson-Dellosa • CD-104624   95

Worksheet 4 (page 96)

Name _____ 6.L.4b, 6.L.6

Greek and Latin Roots

Many English words contain roots from other languages such as Greek and Latin. For example, the word *television* contains the roots *tele* and *vision. Tele* means "distance," and *vision* means "to see." Therefore, a *television* is an object that lets you see things from a distance. Read the list of roots below.

cred: believe	**jud:** law	**crypt:** hidden	**temp:** time
mar: sea	**leg:** read	**aud:** hear	**port:** carry

Use these roots to match the following words with their meanings.

audible	temporary	credible	marine
cryptic	judicial	legible	portable

1. able to be carried **portable**
2. relating to the law **judicial**
3. relating to the sea **marine**
4. able to be believed **credible**
5. lasting for only a short time **temporary**
6. able to be read **legible**
7. mysterious **cryptic**
8. able to be heard **audible**

96   © Carson-Dellosa • CD-104624

© Carson-Dellosa • CD-104624

Answer Key

Name _____

(6.L.4b, 6.L.6)

Greek and Latin Roots

Many English words contain roots from other languages such as Greek and Latin. For example, the word *monorail* contains the roots *mono* and *rail*. *Mono* means "one," so a *monorail* is a vehicle that runs on a single rail. Read the list of roots below.

cap: take, seize	**brev:** short	**ver:** truth	**magn:** large
nomen: name	**alter:** other	**nov:** new	**cogn:** know

Use these roots to match the following words with their meanings.

alternate   recognize   abbreviate   magnify
novice   nominate   verify   captivate

1. to be familiar with   **recognize**
2. to make larger   **magnify**
3. to hold someone's attention   **captivate**
4. to make shorter   **abbreviate**
5. to change between two things   **alternate**
6. to make sure something is true   **verify**
7. to name someone as a candidate for office   **nominate**
8. someone who is new at doing something   **novice**

Name _____

(6.L.4d, 6.L.6)

Decoding Using Word Parts

Compound words are two words that have been joined to form another word. They do not always keep the meanings of both words. For example, a *skyscraper* does not actually scrape the sky. A *skyscraper* is a very tall building. In the chart below, write the literal meaning for each word that makes up the compound word. Then, write what the compound word means.

Compound Word	Literal Meaning for First Word	Literal Meaning for Second Word	Actual Meaning
1. airport	air: what you breathe	port: place for ships to dock	place where planes land
2. jellyfish	jelly: sweet spread for bread	fish: animal that swims	type of sea creature
3. newspaper	news: current events	paper: thin material made from pressed wood	printed paper with current events
4. upstairs	up: vertical direction	stairs: steps	on the floor above
5. playground	play: have fun	ground: earth	place where children play
6. bookkeeper	book: something you read	keeper: one who keeps something	someone who keeps records for a business
7. waterfall	water: liquid that people and animals drink	fall: tumble down	water that flows over a cliff
8. birthday	birth: being born	day: 24 hours	day someone is born
9. popcorn	pop: burst	corn: vegetable	corn that has been popped
10. afternoon	after: later than	noon: twelve o'clock	after twelve o'clock

---

Name _____

(6.L.4d, 6.L.6)

Decoding Using Word Parts

Compound words are two words that have been joined to form another word. They do not always keep the meanings of both words. For example, a *brainstorm* does not actually mean "a storm occurring in the brain." A *brainstorm* is when you think of a lot of ideas for solving a problem. In the chart below, write the literal meaning for each word that makes up the compound word. Then, write what the compound word means.

Compound Word	Literal Meaning for First Word	Literal Meaning for Second Word	Actual Meaning
1. uproot	up: vertical direction	root: part of a plant	to pull up something
2. airplane	air: what something can breathe	plane: flat surface	something that people fly in
3. whirlpool	whirl: spin	pool: body of water	place where water spins downward
4. shortstop	short: not tall	stop: halt	baseball player
5. haircut	hair: something that grows on your head	cut: clip	to get hair clipped
6. clothespin	clothes: something to wear	pin: something that holds things together	pin that holds clothes on a line
7. postcard	post: mail	card: sturdy paper	card you send in the mail
8. supermarket	super: great or large	market: grocery store	large grocery store
9. teacup	tea: something to drink	cup: container	container used to drink tea
10. sailboat	sail: a piece of fabric	boat: small ship	small ship with a sail

---

Name _____

(6.L.4b, 6.L.6)

Decoding Using Word Parts

Portmanteau words were made by combining two words. For example, the word *brunch* was made by combining *breakfast* and *lunch*. Make a new word by combining the words in each row to make a word in the word box. Then, write what the new word means.

Internet   flare   moped   glimmer   motel   smog
motorcade   crunch   splatter   spork   fanzine   sitcom

1. flame + glare = **flare** meaning: **burning light that glows**
2. smoke + fog = **smog** meaning: **pollution**
3. motorcar + parade = **motorcade** meaning: **parade of cars**
4. crispy + munch = **crunch** meaning: **to make noise when eating**
5. motor + hotel = **motel** meaning: **place you can stay overnight**
6. spoon + fork = **spork** meaning: **spoon-like utensil with tines**
7. gleam + shimmer = **glimmer** meaning: **a flickering light**
8. splash + spatter = **splatter** meaning: **to scatter liquid**
9. international + network = **Internet** meaning: **a large computer network linking smaller networks worldwide**
10. fan + magazine = **fanzine** meaning: **magazine devoted to a celebrity**
11. motor + pedal = **moped** meaning: **vehicle with pedals and a motor**
12. situation + comedy = **sitcom** meaning: **comedy TV show**

Answer Key

Name _____ 6.L.5a, 6.L.6

Figurative Language

Read the poem. Then complete the activities.

Winter Sunrise
by J. P. Wallaker

Rose fingernails push back
star-sparkled blanket.

Warm toes slide out,
feel cold morning.

Pink pajama-clad body sits on side of bed,
shivering,
standing,
stretching.

Sparkle . . .
A snow day.

1. To what does this poem compare a sunrise? **someone getting out of bed**

2. Think of a sunrise. Make connections between the poem and an actual sunrise. Write a literal interpretation for each image.

   Fingernails: **the first rays of light**

   Blanket: **the night sky**

   Toes: **more light**

   Body: **the sun**

3. Draw a picture to illustrate the sunrise.
   Check students' drawings.

Name _____ 6.L.5a, 6.L.6

Figurative Language

Sunset
by J. P. Wallaker

Blaze extinguished
Smoldering
Blanket of ash
Speckled with fireflies

Read the poem. Then complete the activities.

1. To what does this poem compare a sunset? **a fire that has been put out**

2. Draw a line from each line in the poem to its literal interpretation.

   Blaze extinguished — the sky graying at dusk
   Smoldering — the stars sparkling across the sky
   Blanket of ash — the sun going below the horizon
   Speckled with fireflies — the pinks, reds, purples, and oranges above the horizon

3. Draw the sequence of events described in the poem. **Check students' drawings.**

   | 1 | 2 |
   | 3 | 4 |

Name _____ 6.L.5a, 6.L.6

Figurative Language

An idiom is a figure of speech. An idiomatic phrase has a different meaning than the literal meaning of the individual words. Circle the best meaning for the underlined idiom.

1. Father asked Yana to be quiet while he was on the phone. Walter was intentionally bothering Yana. Mother told Yana to ignore Walter or she would play right into his hands.
   a. put hands on her shoulders
   b. (fall into a trap that someone plans for ulterior motives)
   c. make noise by playing hand instruments

2. While Zendy was reading her novel, she ran across the date when World War II began.
   a. moved quickly across a library
   b. crossed out the dates
   c. (happened to find information)

3. Adrian thought he was too old to help with the scavenger hunt. Melina told him to let his hair down and join in the fun.
   a. take his hair out of the rubber band
   b. (relax)
   c. get his hands out of his hair

4. We could hardly keep a straight face when Maddie looked at her four-year-old friend and very seriously said, "I believe you should act your age."
   a. (not laugh or smile)
   b. not have any curves or angles
   c. keep the drawing of a face as straight as a line

5. Brett did not tell Chelsea the secret, because he did not want her to let the cat out of the bag.
   a. (tell the secret)
   b. let the kitten (who was a secret) out of his backpack
   c. rip a hole in the tote bag

Congratulations!

receives this award for

_____

_____

Signed _____

Date _____

abbreviate

© CD

abundant

© CD

amplify

© CD

autobiography

© CD

beverage

© CD

astronaut

© CD

bristle

© CD

biologist

© CD

campus

© CD

caption

© CD

certificate

© CD

chronology

© CD

circumstance

© CD

coax

© CD

confident

© CD

completion

© CD

dehydrate	deliberate	demonstrate	disability
distinguish	distribute	emphatic	enchant
equivalent	excel	exhilarating	exquisite
faculty	flexible	fluid	evacuate

© CD

assignment	graduate	gingerly	fragile
© CD	© CD	© CD	© CD
hemisphere	habitat	guarantee	grammar
© CD	© CD	© CD	© CD
initial	immortal	immigrant	identical
© CD	© CD	© CD	© CD
literal	lavish	jostle	intention
© CD	© CD	© CD	© CD

manuscript	maximum	mechanism	metropolitan
miniature	minimum	narrate	megaphone
neutral	nourish	occupation	outlandish
paragraph	partially	perceive	composition

© CD © CD © CD © CD © CD © CD © CD © CD © CD © CD © CD © CD © CD © CD © CD © CD